The Washington Papers/98   Volume XI

U.S. INTERESTS IN AFRICA

HELEN KITCHEN

Published with The Center for
Strategic and International Studies,
Georgetown University, Washington, D.C.

PRAEGER

PRAEGER SPECIAL STUDIES • PRAEGER SCIENTIFIC

Library of Congress Cataloging in Publication Data

Kitchen, Helen A.
   U.S. interests in Africa.

   (The Washington papers, ISSN 0278-937X ; 98, v.11)
   Includes bibliographical references.
   1. Africa—Relations—United States. 2. United
States—Relations—Africa. 3. Africa—Foreign relations
—1960-   . 4. United States—Foreign relations—
1981-   . 5. Africa—Economic conditions—1960-
6. Africa—Strategic aspects. I. Title. II. Title: US
interests in Africa. III. Series.
DT38.7.K57 1983   327.73'06   83-2408
ISBN 978-0-275-91575-9

The *Washington Papers* are written under the auspices of The Center
for Strategic and International Studies (CSIS), Georgetown University,
and published with CSIS by Praeger Publishers. The views expressed in these
papers are those of the authors and not necessarily those of The Center.

Published in 1983 by Praeger Publishers
CBS Educational and Professional Publishing
a Division of CBS Inc.
521 Fifth Avenue, New York, New York 10175 U.S.A.

Contents

iii

Preface

One of the perils of titling a book before copy is in hand is that manuscripts are wayward creatures that sometimes move in unenvisaged directions. Although this contribution to the CSIS *Washington Papers* series is indeed concerned, as stated on the cover, with *U.S. Interests in Africa*, its focus is more precisely identified in the heading of the concluding chapter—"Is a Coherent Africa Policy Possible?"

The slimness of the volume is also somewhat misleading, in that I have synthesized and summarized in these few pages a large body of findings on North and sub-Saharan Africa and the U.S. policymaking process developed and refined over nearly 30 years of monitoring both African affairs and the folkways of Washington, D.C.

Moreover, even 64 footnotes and the many textual references to the works of others cannot convey the extent to which I am indebted to both actors and analysts for their counsel and substantive contributions to this and earlier publications of mine, which have cumulatively broadened and deepened my understanding of the complexities of the issues and relationships discussed.

Some individuals who must be singled out for a special note of appreciation for the time they took from other pressing responsibilities to contribute substance or to critique various segments of this particular publication include Michael Clough, Gerald A. Funk, L. Gray Cowan, David E. Albright, Lucius Battle, Francis A. Kornegay, Jr., J. Wayne Fredericks, Langdon Palmer, Robert Hoen, Manfred Halpern, Carol Lancaster, William Mulligan, I. William Zartman, A.M. Babu, Donald McHenry, Daniel G. Matthews, Bruce Oudes, and my CSIS colleagues Charles Ebinger and William A. Nurthen. The generosity of many friends currently holding policymaking positions in the executive branch of the U.S. government and senior staff positions in the Congress has been essential in assuring relevance and accuracy.

The two persons to whom I am most indebted for keeping this project (and me) on track, however, are Martha Frost ("Moffie") Gordon, whose designations as the administrative assistant for the Center's African Studies Program and as editorial assistant for the monthly *CSIS Africa Notes* do not begin to convey the scope of her human and professional contribution to our every undertaking, and J. Coleman ("Cole") Kitchen, Jr., who coordinates our quite awesome daily take of research materials on Africa's 50-plus entities and is in addition a most meticulous and supportive editor. The writing of this book and other activities of the African Studies Program have also been made more manageable, and have been mellowed, by the assistance of our two student interns, Gerald Holmes of George Washington University and Gerard Sears of Georgetown University, from whom we expect to hear much in the years to come.

January 1983

1

Who Cares About Africa—
And Why?

In the 1980s—as in the 1970s, the 1960s, and the 1950s—
assessments of the interests of the United States in Africa
by those shaping or seeking to shape this nation's foreign
policy remain equivocal. The conflicting signals that come
from various Washington power bases in both the executive
and legislative branches of government and from media
pundits confuse not only Americans but also Africans, European allies, the Soviet Union, and Cuba. The reasons for
the continuing lack of consensus in defining how much of
Africa matters to us, and why, fall into five broad groupings.

The East-West Chessboard Issue

Jousting between various schools of thought represent-
ing different perceptions of Africa's significance has divided Washington policymakers and policy monitors of
both parties and has existed within all departments of the
executive branch since World War II. The major polarizing
issue has been the Soviet Union's emergence on the African

1

scene. "Between those who dismiss the Soviet-Cuban presence as irrelevant and those who view East-West competition
in Africa in simplistic geopolitical terms," I wrote during a
particularly cacophonic period of the Carter presidency in
1979, "there exists a discouragingly small band that sees
the appearance of the USSR, East Germany, and Cuba in
Africa as a challenge of nuanced complexity."[1] As we move
toward the mid-1980s, these three viewpoints can still be
found within various American constituencies, but the battle for primacy in Washington policymaking circles is now
over ways of interpreting and responding to the Soviet challenge. Few voices are raised any longer to dismiss the Soviet-
Cuban presence as irrelevant.

For those who perceive Africa primarily as a segment of
a global East-West chessboard, U.S. national interests in
the continent are largely economic and geopolitical. The economic priorities include retaining access to certain minerals
obtainable from Zaire southward categorized as critical to
defense-related industry and, to a lesser extent, oil. The geopolitical priorities are to deter or counter hegemonic intru-
sions by the Soviets or their surrogates into African countries and regions historically linked to the West, and to ce-
ment "special relationships" with governments willing to
provide access to ports and other facilities supportive of a
global U.S. military outreach.

The centrist pragmatists (sometimes dismissed by critics on the right as "regionalists") differ from the chessboard
school in that they perceive the African environment and issues as more complex, nuanced, and malleable. Their belief
that the most effective way of countering Soviet influence in
Africa is to encourage resolution of the local conflicts that
attract external patrons and arms is based on four crucial assumptions. These are that intrastate and interstate conflict
in Africa arises from indigenous social, political, and economic stresses and from institutional weaknesses; that few,

if any, African conflicts are attributable, solely or even chiefly, to Soviet machinations; that political and military links established between external powers and African governments or liberation movements primarily on a basis of immediate needs and availability are highly labile; and that nationalism and, increasingly, economic concerns are stronger forces in Africa than ideology. Former Secretary of State Cyrus Vance characterized the operational mandate that flows from this set of perceptions of the African scene as affirmative employment of precisely those elements for sustained influence—provision of capital, technological skills, access to export markets—that the Soviet Union is not inclined or able to provide to Africa.

Weakness of Institutional Memory

Much has been made of the fact that Judge William P. Clark, who served as deputy secretary of state before becoming President Reagan's national security adviser, could not name the prime minister of Zimbabwe during his 1981 confirmation hearing before the Senate Foreign Relations Committee. Although this incident made good news copy, Judge Clark's lack of previous attention to the African scene is not as exceptional as it was made out to be. Every change of presidents and each off-year congressional election brings into central policymaking and policy vetting roles a new wave of officials and legislators who may have only a nodding or narrowly focused acquaintance with African issues.

Although Assistant Secretary of State for African Affairs Chester A. Crocker had been educated in the intricacies of African politics more intensively than any preceding political appointee in that State Department post, there was no official in the Reagan administration's foreign policy structure above the assistant secretary level who came to office with a firsthand knowledge of Africa's political history. Compare this with French President François Mitterrand's and External Relations Minister Claude Cheysson's intimate ties with Africa and many of its leaders over decades, or the years of exposure to Africa's ethnic and political subtleties that enabled Lord Carrington, then Britain's foreign secretary, to play the role of midwife for Zimbabwe so brilliantly in 1979.

In May 1978, at a time when leading personalities of the Carter administration and the Congress were engaged in a highly public spate of internecine squabbling over how much blame should be placed on the Soviet Union and Cuba for an invasion launched from Angola by dissident Zairian exiles into their home province of Shaba, British Prime Minister James Callaghan observed during a Washington press conference: "There seem to be a number of Christopher Columbuses setting out from the United States to discover Africa for the first time. It's been there a long time."[2] What Mr. Callaghan seemed to imply was that, although the colonial era relationship between Europe and Africa had been marked by many injustices, it had required the former colonial powers—not only France and Britain, but Portugal as well—to develop a comfortable working knowledge of African history and dynamics.

The weaknesses in institutional memory that derive from our lack of a colonial era presence in Africa are understandable. Less defensible is the low priority given to institutional memory in the "clean slate" approach that, more often than not, characterizes the changes that take place in the policymaking apparatus when presidential power is transferred from one party to another in Washington.

As late as the third year of the Carter administration, it has been noted, no officer serving in the State Department's Office of Southern African Affairs had had prior experience in the country or countries for which he was responsible.[3]

Another striking indication of this dismissal of the importance of institutional memory can be seen in the absence of any substantive consultation, either during the Carter-to-Reagan transitional period or in the year thereafter, between Assistant Secretary of State Crocker and his predecessor, Richard Moose, or with former U.S. Ambassador to the United Nations Donald McHenry, the point man for the five-nation Contact Group on Namibia during the Carter presidency. Even at the career level, there was virtually a complete turnover of those most intimately involved in the complex negotiations regarding Namibia, the African issue to which both the Carter and Reagan administrations accorded highest priority. Of the major officials during the Carter period, only former Ambassador to Zambia Frank Wisner, who subsequently became Crocker's senior deputy, has been a key figure throughout. It is noteworthy, too, that the United States has had four secretaries of state since Namibia became a central U.S. concern in 1977.

This frequent changing of the guard in Washington has been used to good advantage by South Africa, whose negotiating team led by Foreign Minister—and former Ambassador to the United States—Roelof (Pik) Botha has remained substantially intact. The ultimate contrast with the "swinging door" in the U.S. policymaking apparatus is, of course, to be found in Moscow and Havana: Soviet Foreign Minister Andrei Gromyko had dealt with nine different U.S. secretaries of state by 1982 and Cuba's Fidel Castro has been the *bête noire* of seven successive U.S. presidents.

Among the Frontline states and major political movements of southern Africa involved in the Namibia negotiations there has also been a degree of continuity that contradicts the popular image of kaleidoscopic power shifts throughout the continent. Three of the major Frontline participants— Presidents Kenneth Kaunda of Zambia, Julius Nyerere of Tanzania, and Samora Machel of Mozambique—have been heading their respective governments since independence. Angola's José Eduardo dos Santos and Botswana's Quett Masire, close associates of predecessors who died in office, succeeded to the presidency in accordance with pre-established constitutional procedures.

As will be discussed further in Chapter 5, the strengthening and broadening of the permanent bureaucracy's capability and responsibility for understanding the political and economic forces shaping Africa's past, present, and future behavioral patterns should be a high-priority item in any list of U.S. interests in the continent. There are no quick fixes for Africa's problems, and history does not unfold there in neat packages suited to four-year U.S. presidential terms.

Two Bureaus = Two Policies

A third element contributing to mixed signals on Africa is the bureaucratic anomaly that splits responsibility for one of the most volatile areas of the continent between two bureaus of the Department of State. When the Bureau of African Affairs was first established in 1958, its domain included all of Africa except Egypt. In 1974, during the Kissinger era, a decision was made to transfer Algeria, Morocco, Libya, and Tunisia into the Bureau of Near Eastern and South Asian Affairs. Under this rearrangement, the assistant secretary of state for African affairs has responsibility for policy with regard to Chad, the Western Sahara, Sudan, and an Organization of African Unity (OAU) polarized in the early 1980s over Saharan issues. But responsibility for dealing with some of the principals in these areas—Morocco's King Hassan, Libya's Mu'ammar al-Qaddafi, and Algeria's Bendjedid Chadli—falls to a bureau focused on critical matters east of Suez that has little interest in or time for the infinite complexities of Saharan politics.

The Reagan administration's very different styles of operation in northern and southern Africa can be viewed, in part at least, as a manifestation of both the substantive and bureaucratic dualities described above. In southern Africa, one may dispute the specifics but not the conceptual integrity of the policy of "constructive engagement" designed by Assistant Secretary Crocker. Nuanced diplomacy knowledgeably respectful of the domestic pressures on all of the governments and political personalities of the region has been employed in a carefully orchestrated effort aimed at achieving two key objectives: a ceasefire and independence for Namibia that will be honored by all parties and governments and a peaceful withering away (subsequently hardened to "withdrawal of") the Cuban military forces and advisers in Angola. In northern and eastern Africa, in contrast, geostrategic considerations appear to have dictated policy actions that are driven primarily by national security perceptions and the needs of the new Rapid Deployment Force (RDF). In this context, the focus on military-related assistance and arms sales as trade-offs for access to naval and air facilities in these areas of the continent has been regarded as justifiable. The hardening of positions to which the United States is contributing in this region of various stalemated, incipient, and ongoing local wars contrasts sharply with the "honest broker" role the United States has elected to play in southern Africa.

The Safari Tradition of the Media

If U.S. media coverage of Africa is evaluated in terms of relative space allotment and accuracy of basic geographical, economic, and ethnic references and reportage of specific events, the verdict is that significant progress has been made since that day in 1955 when the *Christian Science Moni-*

tor's John Hughes (who became Secretary of State George P. Shultz's press spokesman in 1982) arrived in Africa to become one of only three U.S. correspondents covering the entire sub-Saharan region.[4] But there remains, as a veteran of the African beat has observed, a lingering "safari tradition" in the way American journalism deals with the continent:

> In 1869, James Gordon Bennett of *The New York Herald* sent Henry Morton Stanley off to Africa with these cosmic instructions: "I want you to attend the opening of the Suez Canal and then proceed up the Nile. Send us detailed descriptions of everything likely to interest the American tourists. Then go to Jerusalem, Constantinople, the Crimea, the Caspian Sea, through Persia as far as India. After that you can start looking around for Livingstone. If he is dead, bring back every possible proof of his death."
>
> More than a hundred years later, the American press is still engaged in a voyage of discovery in relation to Africa. In contrast to Britain and France, where journalists have made a prestigious lifetime career of becoming authorities on Africa, an American journalist is expected to approach Africa as a short-term assignment in the safari tradition. The reward for those who explore their domain conscientiously is promotion to an area of greater journalistic (and diplomatic) priority.... [T]he practice of sending talented and innovative generalists to Africa produces the kind of "zingers" that please editors but results in an incomplete mosaic and a lack of institutional memory.[5]

In a column in the *New York Times* in October 1982, Flora Lewis recalled a colleague's query a few years ago about "what ever happened to that war in Eritrea?" Lewis reported that her answer was that the war never went away, the reporters did. "One of the oldest philosophical questions," she observed, "is whether a tree crashing in a forest with no one to hear makes a sound, or whether sound is only what registers on an ear." What we don't know because "the restless spotlight" has moved can still hurt, she warns.[6]

For those of us who follow African developments on a continuing basis, there is no escaping the costly outlay for airmail subscriptions to a range of European as well as African newspapers, weeklies, and news services. Many of the accounts by U.S. newspaper and wire service correspondents are informed and conscientious, but follow-up is inconsistent. What one still gets from the U.S. media in the 1980s are discontinuous segments of the day-to-day history of Africa.

The Changing Composition of "the Africa Constituency"

The limited success of the domestic U.S. "Africa constituency" in shaping U.S. policy over the past 25 years derives in part from organizational and factional problems. But its limited results also stem from the reluctance of leaders of groups forming the angrier activist wing of the constituency to engage in the bread-breaking and other forms of social and political stroking that characterize the operational mode of Washington's most effective foreign policy lobbies (notably Israel's).

Among the groups whose influence on U.S. policy has been limited by a profound ambivalence about how or whether to deal with the Washington power structure are Trans-Africa, the major black U.S. lobby concerned with U.S. policy in Africa and the Caribbean; the church-supported Washington Office on Africa; and the American Committee on Africa based in New York.[7] Other members of the constituency that seek to influence policy through more traditional lobbying techniques and channels—notably the predominantly Democratic Congressional Black Caucus, the Afri-

can-American Institute just left of center, and the newer
Heritage Foundation on the right—have had varying
degrees of entrée and influence, depending on which political party held the White House or controlled the two houses
of Congress.

It is too early to determine what effect some quite bi-
zarre realignments now taking place in the constituency will
have on U.S. policy. At a time when the nuclear freeze issue
and domestic economic stresses are absorbing some of the
energies previously devoted to disinvestment and other an-
tiapartheid campaigns directed toward South Africa, the
Africa constituency has acquired new bedfellows and new
spokesmen from mainstream America. The idea of a tactical
alliance with U.S. multinational corporations galls many
traditional activists, but the reality is that there has developed in the 1980s a greater degree of convergence between
the assumptions of the activists and the corporations about
the relative importance of the East-West dimension in African politics than there has between corporations and government. Although basic differences over such matters as
disengagement vs. constructive engagement in the relationship with South Africa obviously prevent any overt joining
of forces, even on South African issues the differences are
not as clear-cut as they once were. As Francis A. Kornegay,
Jr. observed in a 1982 Habari Special Report on the transition taking place in the constituency:

> Certainly the prospect of a more active corporate consti-
> tuency in African affairs is likely to challenge the
> political maturity and flexibility of leading elements of
> the activist constituency on Southern Africa, especially
> as the corporations are already bypassing this constitu-
> ency to initiate their own dialogue with the current and
> future leaders of black Southern Africa. More to the
> point, the militant anti-Apartheid elements of Africa's
> constituency in America could become increasingly ir-

relevant given the political and economic imperatives of pragmatic survival confronting African nationalists making the transition from armed struggle to political rule, and the increasing need of American businesses to generate working relationships with nations offering critical raw materials and possibilities of large new markets. In short, the complex economic problems that pose difficult political dilemmas to African liberation movements and post-liberation regimes seeking economic as well as political independence defy simplistic protests.[8]

As an example of the new confluence of views, the U.S. corporations and banks most involved in Africa would have few problems with the following basic principles excerpted from a March 1981 "Statement on United States Foreign Policy" issued by the 18 members of the Congressional Black Caucus:

> We find the assumption that the Soviet Union and Cuba are all-controlling forces in the Third World misses the major thrust of a positive Third World policy and is extremely dangerous. We view the most effective weapon against Soviet imperialism as a policy which emphasizes our inherent strengths—our economic and our technological expertise and our commitment to the democratic process and human rights. When our foreign policy has emphasized these strengths through tenacious and creative diplomacy, the results have been significant and positive. The cases of Zimbabwe, the Sudan, Nigeria, and the Dominican Republic are examples.
>
> We must recognize that liberation movements of the Third World have taken assistance from those willing to offer it, and reject East and West domination.
>
> The Congressional Black Caucus believes that the most realistic perspective for a global policy during the latter half of the 20th century is one that recognizes a

North-South as well as an East-West dimension to foreign policy issues. Therefore, we reject as unrealistic and potentially disastrous to American global interest the Reagan Administration's notion that foreign policy issues, especially in the developing world, must be seen primarily in the context of a purely East-West confrontation.

Not only do we do ourselves and the countries of Africa, the Caribbean, and Latin America a disservice by basing foreign policy on this simplistic notion, we do an even greater disservice to our Western allies and Japan who depend far more than the U.S. on Third World raw material and energy resources. . . .

Finally, in the interest of political stability through peaceful change, the Congressional Black Caucus rejects and will oppose any policies toward developing countries that emphasize either overt or covert military intervention aimed at destabilizing established governments or in blocking progressive reform. Hopefully, we will not have to relearn the costly and tragic lessons of Vietnam. . . . [T]he pursuit of a military solution often ignores the opportunity for a political solution and can further polarize the situation, isolating the U.S. from most of the political forces and our friends in a region.[9]

Another indicator pointing toward a broadened and more informed U.S. consensus on the issue of apartheid was a column published in the *Washington Star* on June 10, 1981 under the by-line of Senator Nancy Kassebaum, the Republican chairman of the Senate Foreign Relations Committee's subcommittee on Africa. Expressing concern about the "euphoria in Pretoria" and the "despair in black African capitals" following the major Republican victory in 1980, she challenged as false the "widespread . . . belief among political commentators that the election signaled an American acquiescence to South Africa's institutionalized system of racial oppression." Noting the absence of any areas of compatibility between "mainstream Republican philosophy" and the content and practices of apartheid, she concluded:

> It is ironic that those in South Africa who sound the most like Republicans by demanding the right to private property, the right to be considered for jobs without regard to race, and freedom from government regulation and interference . . . are described as "radical left" and even Marxists. It is also ironic that there is more harmony between the 1980 Republican platform and the decision of the "Marxist" government in Zimbabwe to dismantle a comprehensive system of public housing for blacks and to substitute a system of widespread home ownership (on the basis that the public housing system was "racist") than there is with the South African system.[10]

2

Other External Actors

Since the Department of State's Bureau of African Affairs was created in 1958, nine individuals (six career diplomats and three political appointees) have held the position of assistant secretary of state for African affairs. If the incumbent and former bureau heads were to hold a reunion, it is likely that at least one point on which they would agree is that the only sure way of keeping an African item from sliding off the agenda of the secretary of state's morning staff meeting is to package it with East-West wrappings. Attaining presidential-level attention for an African policy initiative is more complicated and protracted, but establishing a connection between the proposed action and U.S. global concerns—that is, the Soviet Union—is again mandatory.

In the Kennedy-Johnson period, management of the deep involvement of the United States in the civil war that erupted in the former Belgian Congo (now Zaire) shortly after independence was taken out of the bureau and handled by a high-level task force that viewed the conflict and the associated power struggle between various Zairian personalities as an ideological duel that "the West" had to win. In the

Carter-Reagan period, the explanation for the irony that three of Africa's intrinsically less interesting sandboxes—Namibia, Libya, and Somalia—have engaged presidential-level attention is that these three countries, for different reasons, have acquired a new identity as key pieces on the East-West chessboard.

The case of Namibia is of particular interest in this connection. Here, a clear differentiation can be made between the largely nonideological and regional focus of the role the United States has undertaken in leading the many-sided negotiations aimed at ending a dispute that has destabilizing ramifications for all of southern Africa and the particular element that has made it possible to enlist cabinet and presidential-level support for this policy. In both the Carter and Reagan administrations, the presence of 20 thousand or so Cuban troops in neighboring Angola and the Africa Bureau's convincing case that a Namibia settlement would offer a genuine prospect of achieving a peaceful withdrawal of that presence have assured those responsible for implementing the Namibia policy the required clout to deal authoritatively with South Africa as well as the other African governments and movements involved.

It is against this Washington backdrop that the roles of the Soviet Union and Cuba in Africa must be sorted out. Any useful accounting of U.S. interests in the affairs of the continent must go beyond visceral, undifferentiated anti-communism to take a measured look at the Soviet and Cuban presence from other, more analytical, perspectives.

The Soviet Union

An assessment of Moscow's role must differentiate between generalized desires and operational priorities. There is little argument among Kremlinologists about the Soviet Union's aspirations with regard to Africa since the end of the 1950s, when it began to revise its previous perception of the emerging nations of the continent as ripe for "genuine" revolutionary breakthroughs. These aspirations, as of the early 1980s, include validating the USSR's role as a global power; undermining the West's assumed right to paramountcy in economic and political relations with the continent in ways that do not impose heavy economic burdens on Moscow or its allies; and establishing and maintaining the option of future access to Africa's minerals and raw materials. The Soviets also seek to counter and lessen Chinese influence; encourage rivalry and cleavages among the Western powers; establish and maintain equal access with the West to adjacent sea lanes; further the radicalization of black politics, especially in the fluid southern region; and nudge the United States into closer identification with the white rulers of South Africa.

The idea that there is an operative Soviet master plan for achieving these goals is increasingly discounted, however, in part because the record shows that Africa falls somewhere below Europe, East Asia, the southern rimlands of the USSR, and the Middle East in the hierarchy of Soviet geopolitical and resource allocation priorities. Within Africa, contrary to the view from Pretoria, the Horn region seems likely to continue to be of more strategic importance to Moscow than southern Africa.

Sovietologist Seth Singleton's mid-1982 assessment of the Soviet Union's role in southern Africa, like those of most of his colleagues, does not support Pretoria's claim that the Soviet Union is currently mobilizing a "total onslaught" against South Africa. In an introductory passage, he writes:

> The 1975 civil war in Angola provided an opportunity for the Soviet Union to establish its presence and influence in southern Africa, and the Soviets grabbed it. . . .

The Soviets have become an important actor in southern Africa. However, the capability of the Soviet Union and its allies to control the flow of events is limited. The Soviets do not possess means to enforce an *un*-natural alliance in southern Africa. Soviet success depends on African needs for weapons and for the military and internal security training provided by the Soviets and primarily their Cuban and East German allies; weapons and training are all the communist nations can offer. If economic development needs replace those of armed struggle, and if the West provides alternatives to armed struggle. . . . , Soviet influence will wither.[11]

Regarding the ways in which southern Africa is important to Soviet geostrategy and the ways in which it is quite unimportant, Singleton concludes:

Southern Africa is utterly unimportant to Soviet and Socialist Community security. Naval patrols in the south Atlantic and intelligence ships which monitor the flow of supplies and naval activity are useful adjuncts to Admiral Gorshkov's scope of operations but are not worth major risks or much expenditure of political capital or military or economic resources . . . Among the Third World outposts of socialism, Cuba and Vietnam have first claim on Soviet attention and resources, followed by Ethiopia and South Yemen, which are more useful than southern Africa for harassment of Western resource supply. . . .[12]

The Soviet Union's role on the Horn of Africa has been characterized by Robert Legvold as "a curious mixture of success and failure . . . of realpolitik and naivete, of caution and assertiveness."[13] Gerald A. Funk, who has followed the Ethiopian scene from inside and out for many years and served as the director of African affairs on the National Security Council staff during the Carter administration, is more spe-

cific about the cultural impediments faced by Marxism in
the African country that most analysts agree has received
priority attention from Moscow in the 1980s:

> In 1981 and early 1982, Mengistu has been increasingly
> governing Ethiopia in the style and manner of a new
> emperor. Life in Addis Ababa is not too different than in
> the old days. The Soviets and Cubans are in low profile;
> the army is well-organized, well-housed, and well-paid.
> The rains have been good, and plenty of teff grain is
> available on the black market. Ethiopia has joined a mil-
> itary pact with South Yemen and Libya; the Italian For-
> eign Minister has stopped by; Mitterrand's France has
> begun to be friendly; 600 political prisoners have been
> freed; an impossibly ambitious new 10-year economic
> plan has been floated by the United Nations (with a de-
> mand for a more equitable share of total Third World
> aid from all sources); it has been made clear that more
> Western aid and trade is desired (on Ethiopian terms, as
> always). . . . The Ethiopians generally have a marvelous
> contempt for most Europeans and their ideas on how to
> run Ethiopia—obviously preferring the tried-and-true
> personal authoritarian way that has served them so well
> for 3,000 years—but they see the Soviets as an especial-
> ly obtuse lot. It is my prediction that there will be no
> communist party running Ethiopia anytime soon. . . .
> In sum, while Ethiopia's economic prospects run
> from bad to dismal for the next several years, Mengistu
> appears to be firmly in control politically, with internal
> stability at least comparable to that enjoyed by Haile
> Selassie in the late 1960s, before the decline set in. The
> "Somali threat" is under control for now. The Eritrean
> insurgency is certainly not ended but is being brought
> down to manageable levels, and travel to Asmara is
> once again possible. The TPLF in Tigre remains a prob-
> lem, but not a serious threat, especially if Eritrea is es-
> sentially tamed. The EPRP and EDU are unlikely to

pose a significant challenge to Mengistu, unless he is
seriously weakened by some catastrophe. There is no
political agitation going on, other than the usual (albeit
sometimes deadly) politics of the Palace—not even in
COPWE [Commission for Organizing the Party of the
Working People of Ethiopia] or, more to the point, especially not in COPWE.[14]

As for Libya, a recent chronicle of Mu'ammar al-Qaddafi's revolution by John K. Cooley views the Moscow relationship with Qaddafi as even more "conditional" than that
with Ethiopia:

> There remains Qaddafi's prospective new ally, the So-
> viet Union. The USSR, some leading analysts believe,
> could buy much more Libyan oil for itself or allow its
> satellites to buy more than it does now, and then try to
> resell it. This happened in 1980 in a small way, when
> Greece took a total of 850,000 tons of Libyan oil directly
> from the Soviet Union in addition to the 3 million tons
> or so it bought directly from Libya. Still, it is doubtful
> that the Soviets could find enough new buyers for more
> than an insignificant quantity. And the Soviet political
> and strategic partnership with Libya is a conditional
> one, with many ifs and buts. Likewise, neither Qaddafi
> himself, nor his possible successors, seems likely to ac-
> cept any massive Soviet oil purchases because they
> would almost inevitably be linked with unacceptable
> political conditions.[15]

One of the guidelines that emerges from this sampling
of Soviet relations with countries in various parts of the continent is that Africa's institutional fragility should not be
mistaken for political naivete. African leaders of varying
ideological leanings increasingly share a perception that the
interest of the two superpowers in their affairs is only inci-
dentally related to African needs and aspirations and that

both the Soviet Union and the United States can be erratic patrons or allies as they barge hither and yon in ploys directed primarily at outwitting or stalemating the other.

An outspoken African exposition on this point was made in 1978 by Lieutenant General Olusegun Obasanjo, then Nigeria's head of state, at the fifteenth annual OAU summit:

> To the Soviets and their friends, I should like to say that, having been invited to Africa in order to assist in the liberation struggle and the consolidation of national independence, they should not overstay their welcome. Africa is not about to throw off one colonial yoke for another. . . . To the Western powers, I say that they should act in such a way that we are not led to believe they have different concepts of independence and sovereignty for Africa and for Europe. A new Berlin-type conference is not the appropriate response to the kind of issues thrown up by the recent Kolwezi episode [in Zaire]. Paratroop drops in the twentieth century are no more acceptable to us than the gunboats of the last century were to our ancestors.[16]

Obasanjo was equally blunt with his fellow heads of state, asking them to face up to the fact "that we cannot be asking powers to leave us alone while in most cases it is our own actions which provide them with an excuse to interfere in our affairs."

Ambiguities in the Soviet Union's perception of its role and influence in Africa were apparent in the exchanges that took place at a "First American-Soviet Symposium on Contemporary Sub-Saharan Africa" held at the University of California at Berkeley under the joint sponsorship of Berkeley's Institute of International Studies and the Institute of African Studies of the USSR Academy of Sciences, November 10 to 13, 1982. It is a small point, but not without significant implications for the analyst, that each time an Ameri-

can participant identified an African country as "socialist,"
a Soviet colleague promptly intervened to note that the correct term in the African context was "of socialist orientation." Another recurrent theme was that the Soviet Union's
achievement of parity as a world power unequivocally gives
it a right to play a role in Africa, but that Africa is a good place
for Soviet-American cooperation because "it is not critical
for our concerns or yours" and not a place where either the
USSR or the United States wants a "new Congress of Berlin" or a "showdown."

Cuba

Cuba's image in Africa—and Cuba's view of its role in Africa—are also undergoing changes in the 1980s. Havana's new
opportunity to exercise influence in various Central American countries closer to home, acting alone as well as func-
tioning as a Soviet surrogate, is a positive incentive for a
shift of priorities to the Western hemisphere.

Weighing against continued Cuban involvement in Angola are Angola's mixed emotions about the millions of Gulf
Oil's petrodollars that are being paid out year after year for
Cuban troops and technicians, an ambivalence reinforced by
the alternative options that have been suggested by the
West as part of the Namibia negotiations. These alternatives have included encouragement of rapprochement between Luanda and Lisbon and the quiet return to jobs in Angola by a growing number of the Portuguese who left en
masse when colonial rule ended in the mid-1970s, Western
initiatives concerning a possible French military role, and
various bilateral and multilateral economic and security aid
packages. The aid cornucopia took on new dimensions in October 1982, when the governments of Angola and Mozambique at last formally applied to take part in negotiations for

the next (1985–1990) Lomé Convention, which will extend the commercial and development links between the European Economic Community (EEC) and 63 African, Caribbean, and Pacific (ACP) nations. The EEC has held firmly to the position that these countries cannot be aided by EEC funds, even as part of a regional grouping such as the Southern African Development Coordination Conference (SADCC), unless they are Lomé signatories. The Catch-22 problem for Angola and Mozambique has been that they receive significant amounts of security and technical assistance from East Germany, and the Lomé Convention's "Berlin clause" recognizes the Federal Republic of Germany's claim to West Berlin that is disputed by the German Democratic Republic.

These straws in the wind do not change the fact that, as of late 1982, an estimated 30 thousand Cuban military personnel were still serving in Africa at the invitation of various governments. The extent to which these forces threaten or do not threaten U.S. interests is a matter of debate, as is the extent to which mixed policy signals from Washington have caused the Cuban numbers to increase since the mid-1970s. Wayne S. Smith, a career foreign service officer who served as director of the State Department's Office of Cuban Affairs from 1977 to 1979 and as chief of the U.S. interests section in Havana from 1979 to 1982, blames U.S. "myopic diplomacy" for the mushrooming of the Cuban presence. Of the entry into Ethiopia, he writes:

> On November 17, 1977, a high ranking U.S. official claimed a new study revealed a recent, dramatic build-up of Cuban forces in Angola. In fact, no such build-up had taken place. True, an ongoing reduction of Cuban troops had stopped and some had returned to Angola in the spring of 1977 because of tensions with Zaire and an abortive coup in May. The United States had known about and understood the reasons for this development

and had nevertheless opened its Havana interests section in the fall. The Cubans were therefore baffled by the administration's statement; when no explanation was forthcoming, they concluded the episode served an immediate domestic purpose: The Carter administration was striking a tough posture toward Cuba to facilitate passage of the Panama Canal treaties through the Senate.

The Cubans had dealt with the United States in good faith until that point but from the November 17 statement forward, rapprochement went sour. In January 1978 the Cubans went into Ethiopia in force. The conviction that U.S. professions of concern over Angola were hollow probably encouraged the Cubans to underestimate American reaction to the intervention. But in the final analysis, a more substantive error led to their action in Ethiopia. In July 1977 the United States had agreed to supply Somalia with arms. This decision was sensible, for Somalia was breaking away from its Soviet and Cuban patrons. The administration's mistake was in not making absolutely clear to the Somalis that the arms were for defensive purposes only and that the United States would not help them pursue their claim to the Ogaden region of Ethiopia. The Somalis interpreted the arms agreement as support for their irredentist ambitions and shortly thereafter invaded Ethiopia. As in Angola, the Soviets and Cubans were not disposed to permit the United States a cheap victory. They had already lost Somalia through defection; they were determined not to see their Ethiopian ally fall in the wake of a Somali invasion. Hence they decided to commit Cuban troops and Soviet equipment to Ethiopia's defense. The Somali surge was turned back.

The arrival and continued presence of Cuban troops in Ethiopia are counter to U.S. interests, but to call their deployment aggression is to take the situation out of context. Had the United States taken greater care, the Somali invasion and the subsequent Cuban intervention might never have taken place.[17]

In any case, the Cuban relationship with Ethiopia has never been entirely comfortable, in part because language and cultural differences are more of a problem here than in lusophone Angola, but also because Havana has remained uneasy about playing a role in the Mengistu regime's repression of the Eritrean separatist movement and in some other policy areas in which Ethiopian nationalism supercedes ideological commitments. In Ethiopia's disputed Ogaden region, Cuban forces maintain a symbolic presence in major towns and have rarely, if ever, been used in serious military actions.

Another reason why some of the bloom has worn off the Cuban-African connection is that Castro's 1979–1983 tenure as coordinator of the Nonaligned Movement did not elevate him to the role of the Third World's preeminent leader that he envisaged when he hosted the organization's 1979 summit. Such divisive developments as the Soviet intervention in Afghanistan, Vietnam's invasion of Cambodia, and the Iran-Iraq war, along with Cuba's failure to win the Latin American seat it expected to occupy on the Security Council beginning in January 1980, made Castro's turn something less than the power trip foreseen by both friend and foe.[18]

Britain and France

A *Sunday Times* (London) columnist summarized the contrast between Britain's and France's postcolonial role in Africa in these terms in October 1982:

> For Britain, decolonisation meant going away. Some felt humiliated by this retreat; others, after a century of trying to run the world, breathed a half-smothered sigh of relief. Some individuals—businessmen, teachers, clergy—stayed and the Commonwealth has provided a

new diplomatic network. But the old official apparatus was swept away. The French never saw it that way. If the British had been the champion colonisers, the French have proved the great decolonisers.[19]

In fact, barring some unforeseen misstep, it is France—rather than either the Soviet Union or the United States—that will be the most influential external power in Africa for the foreseeable future. Contrary to the expectations of some observers that a Socialist victory in the 1981 elections would presage less French involvement in African politics, the trend has clearly been toward more intensive senior-level attention to a widening range of African relationships. French ministerial travels to Africa and official as well as unofficial visits by African heads of state to Paris in the first year of the Mitterrand era revealed increasing emphasis on building economic and diplomatic links, not only within but also beyond the cluster of francophone states that were formerly French colonies.

The *Economist* has underscored one crucial aspect of French staying power that tends to be underrated by newcomers to the game of Africa-watching:

> The black African economies which have done best since independence include most of the 13 nations in the French African community (CFA), a customs union with a shared currency, whose members are firmly tied to the economy of their former colonial master. For the past two decades the GNP of the CFA's members has grown at twice the black African average. Sound money—with exchange rates pegged to the French franc—has kept big spenders in check, helped to prevent the emergence of cheap-food policies that are now destroying agriculture in much of the rest of the continent and persuaded francophone Africa to use its own resources for growth instead of relying on imports and foreign borrowing.[20]

African recognition of the worth of the CFA monetary connection is newly evidenced by reports that Madagascar and the former Belgian colony of Zaire are now negotiating toward membership in the customs union. Representatives of 36 African governments, including 18 African heads of state, met with President Mitterrand at the ninth Franco-African summit, officially called the Conference of French and African Heads of State, hosted by Zaire's President Mobutu Sese Seko in October 1982.

France, along with West Germany, another actor of increasing importance in Africa, takes issue with the present thrust of U.S. policy in Africa insofar as that policy is associated with an inclination to identify African personalities, governments, and issues in a bipolar East-West context. Arguing that "defending Angola against South Africa and avoiding the division of Ethiopia were not unjust causes," Mitterrand is establishing a rapport with Africans along a wide ideological spectrum—a rapport that is not enjoyed by a United States perceived to be forever rediscovering Africa by bits and pieces, or by a Soviet Union available to fill military vacuums—especially with Cubans and/or for hard cash—but disinclined to commit the economic development aid that would further Africa's eventual self-reliance.

Indications are that France's military presence in Africa (some 14 thousand troops and advisers as of mid-1981) will not diminish but may be employed somewhat differently in the years ahead. Meanwhile, economic realities in France itself and the lingering Gaullist mystique will remain influential in French policy toward the continent, allowing Mitterrand to reaffirm the Socialist party's traditionally strong rhetorical position in support of all measures to end "racist policies in Africa," while honoring various commercial contracts signed with South Africa "in the name of France" by previous governments in fields as controversial as nuclear reactors and enriched uranium. Maintaining domestic sup-

port for this degree of emphasis on Africa will require continued proof of the policy's benefits to the French economy
and avoidance of direct involvement in a major African war.

People's Republic of China

In the 1980s, China is emerging from a relatively quiescent
post-Mao interlude to resume a more active and quite independent role in Africa and the Third World generally. The
aim, according to one interpretation of actions taken at the
twelfth party congress of 1982, is to become "not a competitor
to Washington, Moscow, and Tokyo, but the Goliath of the
world's Davids, the respected Security Council veto-power
voice of the powerless."[21]
    The new role was underscored when China used its Se-
curity Council veto in December 1981 to block the reelection
of Kurt Waldheim as UN secretary general and gave its full
support to the candidacy of Tanzania's Salim Salim. In September 1982, the official *Jornal de Angola* accorded front-
page coverage to the news that Angola and China had agreed
to establish diplomatic relations, a development heretofore
blocked by the embarrassment that China, along with South
Africa, had backed the two guerrilla movements that lost
out to the Soviet-supported Popular Movement for the Liberation of Angola (MPLA) in the three-way power struggle
at the time of Angola's independence in 1975. Prime Minister Zhao Ziyang carried forward the policy with a month-
long 11-nation African tour beginning in December 1982,
the culmination of careful groundwork laid on the continent
by four new vice foreign ministers.
    Other recent major developments have included an offi-
cial opening in 1982 of the multimillion dollar Fenola Dam
project in Somalia, abandoned by the Soviets in 1977, and
negotiation of a $24 million aid package with Somalia. Mean-

while, China's most ambitious undertaking in Africa—the $400 million railway completed in 1975 to link landlocked Zambia to Tanzania's port of Dar es Salaam—is being overhauled.

Africa first became a focus of interest during the initial conference of nonaligned nations held in 1955 in Bandung, Indonesia, but the energetic Africa policy highlighted by the visits to the continent of Premier Chou En-lai in 1963–1964 and Foreign Minister Ch'en Yi in 1965 lapsed during the Cultural Revolution. In 1970, China reemerged as a major influence in Africa, and the continent was an arena of intense Sino-Soviet rivalry through most of the decade. As of 1977, China had offered a cumulative total of nearly U.S. $2.5 billion in economic credits and grants to 34 different African countries—a figure representing some 55 percent of all its aid commitments to the non-Communist world.[22] Between 1971 and the end of 1982, some 40 senior-level African delegations led by heads of state paid official visits to China.

Portugal

In 1975, after 14 years of war that demoralized its armed forces and toppled the authoritarian regime of Marcello Caetano, Portugal ended four centuries of colonial rule in Africa. A drift back to Africa began at the end of the 1970s, and the early 1980s were marked by visits to former colonies by President António Ramalho Eanes, Prime Minister Francisco Balsemão, and entourages of businessmen. President Eanes sent a warm message of support to the heads of state of Portugal's five former colonies—Angola, Mozambique, Guinea-Bissau, Cape Verde, and São Tomé and Príncipe—gathered for a third post-independence lusophone summit in Cape Verde in September 1982.

Although Lisbon has not been directly involved in the Namibian independence negotiations, there has been increasing speculation that Portuguese troops, technicians, and professionals might be available to supplant some of the Cubans whose departure from Angola had become by 1982 a South African (and Reagan administration) condition for a settlement. A more specific and overt focus of Portuguese attention, however, has been Mozambique.

Under an agreement worked out in Lisbon in October 1982, Portugal is to become Mozambique's second largest military supplier after the Soviet Union. A formal defense treaty scheduled to be signed in 1983 would make Mozambique the major purchaser of Portuguese arms and would also provide for counterinsurgency training for Mozambican officers in Lisbon and possibly for the seconding of Portuguese instructors to Mozambique. The dual object is to lessen President Samora Machel's dependence on his Soviet bloc allies and to help repel the growing threat to his government posed by the South African-backed rebels of the Mozambique National Resistance (MNR). Meanwhile, Lisbon is facilitating the flow to Maputo of managerial expertise, equipment, technical instructors, and marketing skills to assist in the restructuring of run-down textile and other plants.

The *Financial Times* of London concluded a November 1982 report on Portugal's new role as mentor rather than overlord in Africa with the observation: "Given the many debts owed by Angola and Mozambique to the Comecon bloc, which rushed in when the West shied away, Portugal's relations have charted a careful course. The imminent accession of Angola and Mozambique to the Lomé Convention . . . shows how much distance has been covered since independence in 1975, when the West was their avowed enemy."[23]

3

The Economic Dimension

Leading from Strength

Given the fact that successive administrations in Washington since the 1950s have perceived the limiting of Soviet influence on the governments and military establishments of the continent to be a priority U.S. interest, a first question to be asked is why African doors are opened to Moscow and its helpers. If the French government is correct in its assessment that there are fewer Africans today who see Marxism as the answer to their country's or their continent's problems than there were in the 1960s, we must consider the African needs and interests to which Moscow has more capability and freedom to respond than the West, and specifically the United States. The most obvious answer, of course, is arms.

Among the reasons that arms have been used more extensively than other wooing options that the Soviet Union might have chosen are these:

1. There has been a growing inclination on the part of beleaguered African governments to see force as a necessary means of dealing with domestic political, economic, and

social stresses as well as with regional threats. In addition, movements pressing for majority rule in territories not yet "decolonized"—in Angola, Mozambique, and Zimbabwe in the 1970s, and in Namibia still in the 1980s—give arms priority over all other concerns.

2. The complexities and publicity surrounding the decision-making process in Washington, especially the watchdog role of a Congress responsive to public opinion on foreign entanglements, will always restrict the degree to which the United States can be expected to become involved in any African situation involving arms. The exceptions have been, and are likely to continue to be, situations in which there is a politically marketable ideological (that is, East-West) dimension.

3. The Soviet Union has been since the early 1970s the largest producer of conventional arms in the world and has demonstrated few qualms about transferring even obsolescent weaponry to Third World governments or movements. Soviet military deliveries to sub-Saharan Africa alone climbed to over $3.1 billion in the 1975–1979 period, as compared with $410 million during 1956–1974.[24] Cash-on-the-barrelhead (as in the cases of Zambia and Libya) is always the preferred arrangement, and ideological affinity does not necessarily make the terms easier. According to *Africa Confidential* of London, "Ethiopia's balance of payments deficit ... has grown inexorably since the revolution, with about $2 billion owed [by 1982] to the Soviet Union."[25] The critical factor governing Soviet trade, aid, and the dispatch of military advisers and matériel to Africa is the expressed requirement of governments and other entities in Africa for such interaction.

If we adhere to the working principle that it is better to lead from strength than from weakness, it is clear that, by the very nature of its society and governmental processes, the United States cannot compete with the USSR in arming states or political movements in Africa. U.S. strength vis-à-vis the USSR lies in the role the United States can play—and the Soviets cannot—in helping Africa develop its economic potential and coherence and thus its self-reliance.

Given the present economic constraints within the Soviet Union (Western observers estimate overall economic growth for the rest of the decade at no more, and perhaps substantially less, than 3 percent annually), it is reasonable to predict that the economic dimension of Soviet relations with Africa will not grow significantly in the 1980s. Recent calculations show that Soviet economic aid credits to sub-Saharan Africa for the entire 1970–1979 period were only $269 million (of which $95 million went to Ethiopia). In 1978 and in 1979, the USSR's trade turnover with the sub-Saharan region constituted only 0.8 percent of its total trade turnover with the outside world. Soviet exports to the region ran 0.8 and 0.6 percent of all its exports in the same two years; its imports from there were 0.8 and 1.2 percent respectively.[26]

In contrast, U.S. bilateral aid and trade figures are significantly higher and are well beyond the Soviet reach if one includes U.S. contributions to the major international financial institutions (see Tables 1 and 2). What is lacking in our approach to aid and trade with Africa is any evidence of a conceptual long-term U.S. commitment to Africa's trade and development requirements that would permit us to be viewed as a serious and reliable partner. At least one major reason for this lack of long-term thrust is the constitutional requirement for the executive branch annually to debate internally and then sell to Congress both the concept of aid and a country-by-country justification for the year's package proposal. The principle that applies to other areas of the world and other government programs also applies to Africa: the executive proposes and the Congress disposes. And, with respect to foreign aid, Congress seems to do so with increasing reluctance.

Weaknesses of U.S. Economic Intelligence

The United States is also handicapped in developing a coherent policy toward Africa in the economic area by the scarcity and uneven quality of information and analysis available to government policymakers.

The data problem begins, of course, in Africa itself, where institutional weaknesses, limited financial resources, other priorities, and shortages of administrative and economic expertise continue to hinder the development of basic statistical materials. Even the data available are underutilized, however, because of the limited number of offices and officers in the U.S. government responsible for economic research and analysis regarding Africa.

Dr. Carol Lancaster of Georgetown University, drawing on a range of experience in both the executive and legislative branches of the government, including a stint as deputy assistant secretary for economic relations in the State Department's Bureau of African Affairs during the Carter administration, outlined the dimensions of the problem at a conference ("How to Look at Africa in the 1980s: Information for Decision Makers") hosted by the Defense Intelligence School in September 1982:

> While the intelligence agencies and the Bureau of Intelligence and Research of the Department of State produce policy relevant studies of high quality on African political issues, comparable analyses of economic issues are rare. . . . Books and articles drawn from academic sources are often of limited use for policymakers. Many

TABLE 1
U.S Aid to Sub-Saharan Africa
($ millions)

	1980[a]	1981[a]	1982[b]	1983[c]
Bilateral Economic				
Development				
Assistance	275	300	328	323
PL-480				
Title I	140	147	147	117
Title II	153	175	175	75
Economic Support				
Fund	133	162	163	325
Refugee Aid	14(+90)[d]	12(+94)[d]	12(+107)[d]	NA
Total	715	796	825	840
Percentage Increase	(47%)	(11%)	(4%)	(2%)
Multilateral Economic				
World Bank Total	590	859	962	NA
(U.S. share)[e]	138	198	215	NA
International De-				
velopment Associa-				
tion (IDA) Total	957	954	840	NA
(U.S. share)[e]	315	291	283	NA
African Develop-				
ment Fund	273	311	NA	NA
(U.S. share)[e]	22	31	NA	NA

TABLE 1 (*continued*)
U.S. Aid to Sub-Saharan Africa
($ millions)

	1980[a]	*1981*[a]	*1982*[b]	*1983*[c]
Total U.S. Share of Multilateral Aid[e]	475	520	NA	NA
Total U.S. Bilateral and Multilateral Aid	1,190	1,316	1,323[f]	NA
Percentage Increase	(43%)	(11%)	(1%)	NA
U.S. Military Assistance				
Foreign Military Sales (FMS)	75	78	133	234
International Military and Educational Training (IMET)	3	4	6	9
Total	78	82	139	243
Percentage Increase	(160%)	(5%)	(70%)	(75%)

Sources: Department of State, U.S. Agency for International Development (AID), World Bank, African Development Bank/Fund.
a. Actual.
b. Estimate.
c. Request.
d. Figure in parentheses shows additional assistance rendered through the High Commissioner for Refugees.
e. Imputed from share of total agency resources devoted to Africa.
f. Excludes African Development Fund.

TABLE 2
U.S. Trade with Africa

Country	U.S. Imports from from Africa ($ millions FAS*)		U.S. Exports to Africa ($ millions FAS)	
	1980	1981	1980	1981
Algeria	$6,576.8	$5,038.1	$541.8	$717.3
Angola	527.3	904.1	111.3	268.3
Benin	—	.5	14.9	18.7
Botswana	87.2	131.6	6.0	6.4
Burundi	40.3	28.0	2.9	3.8
Cameroon	604.8	625.4	93.3	152.1
Central African Republic	8.6	6.4	.7	.8
Chad	—	(Z)	1.9	.8
Congo	90.5	287.6	21.8	25.0
Djibouti	—	—	11.6	7.2
Egypt	538.5	397.3	1,873.6	2,159.4
Equatorial Guinea	(Z)	.2	.1	.7
Ethiopia	86.8	83.0	71.9	62.2
Gabon	278.3	431.9	48.1	128.0
Gambia	.2	.4	4.5	3.5
Ghana	206.1	245.5	126.6	153.6
Guinea	75.0	95.8	33.9	53.0
Ivory Coast	288.0	344.4	184.7	129.7
Kenya	53.6	51.8	141.1	150.3
Lesotho	.1	.1	7.8	8.7
Liberia	127.7	113.1	113.1	128.4
Libya	8,594.7	5,300.9	508.8	813.4
Madagascar	90.8	69.3	7.4	16.2
Malawi	25.4	61.6	3.7	5.0
Mali	.4	.9	6.8	5.0

Table 2 (*continued*)
U.S. Trade with Africa

Country	U.S. Imports from from Africa ($ millions FAS*)		U.S. Exports to Africa ($ millions FAS)	
	1980	1981	1980	1981
Mauritania	.4	.2	20.1	26.9
Mauritius	49.7	19.7	21.7	18.2
Morocco	35.3	36.2	344.4	429.0
Mozambique	104.8	83.1	69.1	35.0
Namibia	3.6	7.6	14.2	12.9
Niger	—	(Z)	19.8	12.3
Nigeria	10,905.1	9,249.0	1,149.6	1,522.7
Rwanda	67.5	40.5	5.4	6.2
Senegal	8.9	1.4	41.1	42.3
Seychelles	.6	.4	3.1	3.9
Sierra Leone	77.0	45.0	20.8	26.3
Somalia	.4	.2	55.8	58.8
South Africa	3,320.5	2,445.3	2,463.5	2,911.7
Sudan	17.3	58.0	142.5	208.4
Swaziland	58.5	65.6	6.5	7.2
Tanzania	31.8	18.8	61.7	47.7
Togo	15.9	9.2	19.1	24.2
Tunisia	59.9	10.4	173.5	222.2
Uganda	125.8	101.0	11.6	6.8
Upper Volta	.3	.1	20.3	22.2
Zaire	360.6	423.4	155.0	141.3
Zambia	199.8	113.6	98.5	68.3
Zimbabwe	38.9	109.0	18.8	32.4
Total	$33,783.7	$27,055.6	$8,874.4	$10,904.4

Source: Department of Commerce
* = free alongside ship
(Z) = less than $500,000

are too technical, too theoretical, and sometimes too ideological (or, perhaps, too ideologically different) to be policy relevant. Even the best of academic materials frequently provide too much depth for a policymaker with little time (and often little patience) to digest and reflect on the basic assumptions. Decision makers are usually confronting problems where the options for decision are narrowly defined by the broad policy thrusts and commitments of the administration in power. What is needed is simple, concise background information and analysis, and an evaluation of realistic policy alternatives. Although such analyses should reflect a familiarity with scholarly opinion, the kind of writing required is probably best done by government intelligence and research agencies and, occasionally, by outside consultants.

Compounding the problems of information and analysis is the rarity of economic expertise on the part of decision makers, including those involved in economic policymaking. The exposure to economics of many foreign service officers working on economic issues is too often limited to courses at the Foreign Service Institute. This lack of expertise is not a poor reflection on the officers, but rather a reflection of the relatively low priority assigned to economic issues in U.S. foreign policymaking generally. Economic issues—by their nature, usually involving long-term considerations—are seldom considered at a high level until they have reached crisis proportions and threaten important U.S. interests. This approach sets a priority on political issues which permeates the government foreign policy apparatus. Lower level officers will choose to work on issues, seek positions, and follow career paths which offer the greatest visibility, excitement, and opportunity for advancement.

Another element influencing the low priority assigned to foreign economic policy issues relates to the nature of those issues and the organization of the U.S.

government for dealing with them. Many foreign economic issues involve powerful domestic interests and
groups in a way that diplomatic and political issues do
not. . . . Indeed, as a result of the heavy domestic components of these issues (and possibly the distrust by domestic pressure groups of State Department sympathies and
capabilities in dealing with such issues), operational responsibility for many economic issues has over recent
years been removed from the Department of State and
dispersed among a variety of executive branch agencies.
Economic decision-making has become more complex
and more time consuming.

Since economic issues are a rising concern of
African governments, and directly impact on political
trends and developments throughout the continent,
there is a growing need for U.S. government decision
makers to understand the economic problems facing
Africa and how they affect U.S. interests. If policy for-
mulation is to be ahead of crises rather than reactive
after the fact, we urgently need to direct more research
and analytical attention to this aspect of our interaction
with Africa.

There were indications by the last quarter of 1982 that
the tenure of Secretary of State George P. Shultz, an economist and academician by profession, would be marked by
an upsurge in attention to the interlocking relationship between the traditional areas of foreign diplomacy and economic issues.

Strategic Minerals and Related Concerns

The heavy reliance by the United States and other industrial
democracies on minerals imported from the region south from
Zaire raises new policy problems and choices in the 1980s.

Concern about continued access focuses particularly on South Africa, which dominates world exports of four minerals (chromium, manganese, vanadium, and platinum) that have both industrial and military significance. South Africa is generally credited with having two-thirds of the non-Communist world's known reserves of chromite and vanadium, a third of the manganese, four-fifths of the platinum, and half of the gold. The importance of these reserves to the West is underscored by the fact that the Soviet Union is the principal alternative source of gold, vanadium, and platinum, and an important alternative source of manganese.

Opinions differ on the effect of an interruption of supply from this area of Africa and on the likelihood of such an interruption.[27] Although recent authoritative surveys suggest that American dependence on southern African minerals is not absolute or final (for example, stockpiles could fill the gap while other sources or more costly substitutes are brought on line), the effect on Western Europe and Japan would be acute and lasting.

Andrew M. Kamarck, former director of the Economic Development Institute of the World Bank, has contributed a new perspective on the strategic minerals issue and helped document the long-term interest of the United States in Africa's overall economic development in an unorthodox article, "The Resources of Tropical Africa," published in 1982.

Elaborating on his opening statement that "The most important fact about the natural resources of tropical Africa is that we are still profoundly ignorant about them," Dr. Kamarck reminds us:

> The tropical climate still inhibits the discovery of mineral resources. Although there is no rational basis for believing that countries in the tropics have poorer or fewer mineral resources than those in the temperate zones, a relatively small portion of the known reserves

of the world's minerals has in fact been found so far in tropical countries.

Contrary to current popular assumption, the total mineral resources of the world are enormous. "Known reserves," the figures quoted in nontechnical discussions, are but a tiny fraction of the total of any mineral in existence, for it is not worthwhile to explore for minerals, and go through the process of boring, sinking shafts, and taking and analyzing samples on any mineral occurrence that is not likely to be utilized within a manageable span of years. The U.S. Geological Survey estimated, for example, that at the current world rate of consumption, there are around 840 million years of copper in the world's crust. Even supposing that only one tenth of one percent of the amount in the top one kilometer of the earth's crust is ultimately recoverable, there are still 340 years of world consumption of copper available. However, the figure for known reserves in 1974 amounted to only forty-five years consumption. Briefly, the size of the known reserves estimate depends not only on the knowledge of the existence of a given mineral, but also on the willingness and ability of governments and investors to spend money to prospect for and to prove a deposit, the technology available to bring the mineral to market, and the price at which it can be sold.[28]

In another passage that relates to U.S. interests, including long-term concerns about strategic minerals availability, Dr. Kamarck speaks of the constraints that are imposed on African development by the inadequacy of the continent's transport network:

The scarcity of natural harbors; the lack nearly everywhere of navigable river access to the interior; the African plateau, cut by deep valleys, that dominates most of tropical Africa and makes the building of roads and rail-

ways very costly; the fierce tropical rains that threaten
the rapid erosion of road and railways—all require
massive investment in transport facilities if any ap-
preciable volume of cargo is to be moved. The result is
that even on those rare occasions when a particular mineral can be exploited with a relatively small investment
in the mine, the total investment is likely to be high—
often in the range of hundreds of millions of dollars—
because of the need to invest in a railroad, road, or port.[29]

Oil

A study to be published in 1983 on the economic and political implications of sudden oil wealth in a range of West African countries makes the same basic point regarding Africa's
oil resources that Kamarck has dramatized with regard to
the continent's mineral wealth.[30] If the U.S. Geological Survey could report in the 1880s that little if any oil of commercial value would be found in California or Texas, then it is
not surprising that even as late as 1980 the projections for
West Africa referred to only a "modest potential" for the
Ivory Coast and ignored Equatorial Guinea entirely.

By 1982, the West African countries with significant
proved reserves numbered eight: Nigeria with 16.5 billion
barrels at the top of the list followed by Angola, Congo, Came-
eroon, Gabon, Ivory Coast, Zaire, and Ghana. Exploration
efforts under way in the region have generated projections
that by 1990 not only Ivory Coast, Ghana, and Cameroon
but also Benin and Equatorial Guinea could be producing
at rates from 15 thousand barrels a day (b/d) to 360 thousand b/d. Some World Bank and other analysts go so far as
to estimate that as much as 80 percent of Africa's petroleum
reserves remain to be discovered and that discoverable
reserves on the continent and offshore over the next 20

years could reach 51.3 billion barrels, or 14 percent of worldwide discoveries in the same period.

Although these projections generate hopes of economic takeoffs in countries formerly regarded as destined for permanent marginality (as was Libya when it became independent in 1951), the extent to which this optimism is justified will depend in good part on what has been learned from the problems other Third World nations have encountered in using new oil wealth to achieve sustained and balanced development.

In West Africa, Nigeria stands out as the classic example of what has come to be called "the oil syndrome." In pre-oil days, its real gross domestic product (GDP) was growing at an annual rate of 4.5 percent, agriculture was the leading economic sector, and Nigeria was one of the world's largest exporters of peanuts, palm oil, and cocoa. The manufacturing sector had grown from 1 percent of GDP in 1950 to 5 percent in 1964. Following the 1967–1969 civil war, which significantly dislocated both the manufacturing and agricultural sectors, oil income rose dramatically—from $189 million in 1964 to almost $24 billion in 1981. This rapid influx of foreign exchange and the massive increase in funds available to the government for public spending set in motion a self-perpetuating cycle of hyperinflation. Maintenance of an unrealistically high exchange rate for the naira allowed imports to flood the market at prices lower than domestic producers could meet and remain solvent. Meanwhile, thousands of Nigerians were abandoning the farming areas every year to seek the higher paying jobs that were available in the cities. By 1980, oil earnings accounted for over 90 percent of Nigeria's foreign exchange, and agriculture had shrunk from 58 percent of total GDP in 1964 to 20 percent. From a position of food self-sufficiency, this largely rural nation had slipped into a significant dependency on food imports (over $2.2 billion annually as of the early 1980s). Correcting this situation is now a major government priority, but it will take time.

Although not all African oil producers have suffered the "oil syndrome" as acutely as Nigeria (Cameroon and Algeria are two notable exceptions), the risks remain great that an oil bonanza will not lead to greater economic independence and political stability but to less. Both short and long-term U.S. and African interests can be served by Africa's exploitation of its oil resources. Imports of African oil reduce U.S. dependence on the oil fields of the ever-sensitive Middle East. The Africans gain hard currency that can be used to finance development programs and access to technological know-how. Another longer-term dimension can be added to the mutuality of African and Western interests in this area if more attention is given than has been the case in the past to reinforcing the growing recognition by African governments that oil wealth is a mixed blessing if it is not employed to develop the nation's social fabric.

Africa and the World Monetary Crisis

The "Chicken Little" school of commentators on the crisis that the world monetary system is experiencing has generally misread the African debt picture. The fact that Africa (for reasons that go back to the illogical way in which the continent was carved up at European bargaining tables in the nineteenth century) contains more than 50 nations explains the alarming statistic that it accounts for the largest number of governments caught up in the debt rescheduling merry-go-round.

But if one looks at the numbers more closely, Africa's general debt picture is decidedly less immediately alarming than that of Latin America and a number of Asian countries—in both total debt and debt service ratio. (This latter is the percentage of foreign exchange annually required to pay principal and interest due on foreign debt, defined as official debt with maturities in excess of one year.)

Of a total world external debt of something over $800 billion, the nations of Africa together account for only about 10 to 12 percent, not a great deal more than Mexico alone and roughly the same as all of the nations of Eastern Europe combined. For example, Mexico and Brazil each have an external debt in round figures of $80 billion, Argentina $40 billion, and Chile and Venezuela $15 billion each. The debt service ratio runs 120 percent for Brazil, 130 percent for Mexico, 180 percent for Argentina, 115 percent for Chile, and 95 percent for Venezuela. By contrast, approximate figures for 13 individual nations of Africa as roughly calculated for this study by officials of three major U.S. banks are as follows:

Country	Foreign Debt (including undisbursed debt)		Debt Service Ratio
Algeria	$19	billion	48 percent
Egypt	$15	billion	23 percent
Morocco	$13	billion	38 percent
Nigeria	$12	billion	13 to 19 percent
Ivory Coast	$ 7	billion	33 percent
Zaire	$ 5	billion	37 percent
Tanzania	$ 2	billion	19 percent
Kenya	$ 3	billion	17 percent
Cameroon	$ 2.5	billion	10 percent
Madagascar	$ 1.5	billion	35 percent
Ghana	$ 1.5	billion	11 percent
Congo	$ 1.5	billion	14 percent
Sudan	$ 5	billion	NA because of recent rescheduling

Although these figures, and other data, indicate that few countries in Africa fall into the "overborrowed" category, there is reason for concern that the international financial community will tighten lines of credit to the relatively underborrowed African nations in an effort to stave off the collapse of the dozen or so high debt service ratio countries in Latin America, Asia, and Eastern Europe accounting for roughly half of the world debt. This would create even more service liquidity problems for the continent. It is with regard to this prospect that U.S. long-term interests come into play.

Other Realities—
and Red Herrings

The litany of Africa's economic problems is by now familiar. In the two decades between 1960 and 1980, according to World Bank figures, per capita income in 19 countries grew by less than 1 percent per year, and between 1970 and 1980 a total of 15 countries recorded a negative growth of income per capita. Of the 33 countries listed in the Bank's *World Development Report, 1982* as having a per capita gross national product (GNP) of less than $410, almost two-thirds are African. The increase in food production dropped from 2 percent per year in the 1960s to 1.5 percent in the 1970s; and since population has been rising rapidly (by an annual average of 2.7 percent in the 1970s), food production per person has actually declined. One result of this development is that imports of food grains alone (wheat, maize, rice) have risen by some 9 percent per year since the early 1960s.

As these statistics have mounted, there has been a growing tendency to despair of Africa's economic prospects and to lay all of the blame on "mismanagement" and "corruption." This is as simplistic as the earlier inclination of African governments to lay all of the blame for their faltering economies at the feet of the former colonial powers. Mismanagement at the policy level, misallocation of limited human resources, and uneven implementation of policies adopted in principle are indeed significant reasons for the varying performance records among the African states.

The most serious problems now confronting the continent, however, are related to the dislocation in the world economy triggered by the successive oil shocks of 1973 and 1978, to a long-term and systemic decline in demand for most of the agricultural and mineral raw material exports upon which Africa depends for disproportionate levels of both gross national product and foreign exchange, and to a series of extended droughts, which, coupled with high rates of population growth, have made it increasingly difficult for many African nations to feed themselves. As Dr. Adebayo Adedeji, the Nigerian executive secretary of the UN Economic Commission for Africa, summarizes the requirement to view the crisis in context, Africa is "the least economically developed of all continents, the most dependent on the industrialized market economies, and therefore the most vulnerable to any setback in these economies."[31]

As in any severe recession, the newer, smaller, and undercapitalized enterprises experience the most difficulty, but in the general tightening of international markets, even the more viable enterprises (for example, Nigeria, Ivory Coast, Cameroon, and Gabon) could suffer equally with the poorer or flagrantly mismanaged ones. U.S. policymakers and critics should give priority attention to understanding all of the dimensions of Africa's economic crisis; to do otherwise is to contribute to a self-fulfilling prophecy of nonrecovery.

The Importance of the World Bank and the
International Monetary Fund (IMF)

Approximately 40 African nations are running current account deficits totaling about $9 billion. With bilateral aid more or less level in recent years and usually tied to narrowly described projects, the shortfall has been made up by borrowing from the international financial markets and by the IMF and the World Bank. As the banking system begins a slowdown in lending to the less developed countries (LDCs), a new burden is falling on the World Bank and the IMF. This is occurring at a time when the Bank, while committed to providing an increased share of its long-term soft loans to sub-Saharan Africa, finds itself with less money to disburse than planned as a result of a train of events set in motion by U.S. ambivalence about multilateral aid.

In 1980, under the Carter administration, the United States pledged $4.1 billion over three years to replenish the Bank's "soft window," the International Development Association (IDA). Sixteen other donor nations agreed to supply roughly double that amount, allowing for an anticipated availability of $4.1 billion in 1982. Budget cutting by the Reagan administration threatened to cut 1982 availability back to $2.6 billion, as other donors moved to follow the U.S. lead. Although 1982 funding has been raised back to $3 billion, with all of the other 16 donor states deciding to meet their full obligations regardless of U.S. action, the Reagan administration's cutbacks and its aggressive policy of greater reliance on the private sector are having restrictive effects on both the Bank and the IMF at a time when these institutions are crucial to Africa's economic future and when the private sector is becoming increasingly cautious.

The IMF was not designed, of course, to engage in development assistance, but rather to help out with short-term liquidity problems arising out of balance of payments and exchange rate difficulties. In Africa, however, it has been edging toward developmental support. In 1978, there were only two African nations with IMF credit agreements. In 1982 there were 21, involving nearly half of the continent and $4.5 billion; the list will be longer by the end of the decade.

The relationships between African governments and the IMF are not always smooth, and most of the stresses arise over the tradition of insistence on "conditionality"— the codeword for requiring nations to meet certain standards in fiscal and monetary housekeeping defined by the IMF. Typically, the IMF insists on a tough package of currency devaluation to promote exports, a cut in the now endemic basic food subsidies (and a rise in prices paid to the farmers, to encourage a return to food self-sufficiency), and a general reduction in government spending, on the assumption that a lot of "fat" and corruption can be squeezed out and that a more sound set of national priorities will be established.

Because these conditions present difficult and potentially destabilizing political decisions for governments in the short run, they are often resented and often circumvented. African political leaders (who, like politicians everywhere, tend to live in a short-term universe) argue that the validity of the basic IMF assumption about the effectiveness of the price mechanism in the economic allocation of resources is less applicable to Africa than it is to the developed and developing industrial nations and that cultural, kinship, and indigenous political relationships must be given greater consideration. The IMF's insistence on "conditionality" has in fact occasioned severe political disturbances in a number of countries, and the ability of a government to "survive the IMF riots" is a new political factor that must be taken into account by Africa's decision makers. There is also a strong current of opinion among African and other Third World leaders that, one way or another, the severely declining terms of trade experienced by most African nations need to be addressed as part of a fundamental restructuring of the world's system of trade and finance.

Still, until or unless something better is devised, the World Bank and the IMF system will be seen by Africa as its best immediate hope for assistance during a period of world stagnation. It is important for U.S. politicians to take into account, as they continue to debate the degree of support the United States should give to these institutions, that an increasingly nervous international banking community does seem to be willing to remain positively engaged on the African continent as long as the World Bank and the IMF system remains similarly engaged. If the Bank and the IMF were to cut back their involvement in Africa, a parallel pullback by the private international banking community could be expected.

A New "Bretton Woods"?

The problems of an African nation faced with a 35 percent drop in commodity export prices and a fuel bill reaching one-half or two-thirds of its world exchange earnings are not going to be solved by IMF conditionality alone—any more than the problems of shattering unemployment levels in a depressed U.S. steel industry will be solved by triggering a mini trade war with Japan and Europe.

Perhaps a new Bretton Woods conference or something comparable is needed to redefine the rules of the game. At the very least, it seems time to examine worldwide problems in global terms and for the leaders of the Organization for

Economic Cooperation and Development (OECD) nations to give consideration to new economic ideas before an international economic trauma forces them to do so.

In the interim, U.S. long-term interests in Africa would be well served by an immediate increase in the working capital of the IMF (some economists suggest the creation of a $10–$20 billion emergency fund), followed by a substantial general increase of quotas for a total capitalization of something in excess of $125 billion. The present $67 billion capital, which represents only about 4 percent of world imports as opposed to 12 percent in the early 1960s, is inadequate for the task the IMF is being asked to perform. As one leading international banker phrases it, "we can no longer afford to respond to city-size problems with country-bank capital." Such an increase would give the IMF a great deal more leverage in dealing with major problems such as Mexico and Brazil and also with the requests in Africa and elsewhere for debt rescheduling. If it is in the U.S. interest to keep U.S.-Soviet competition located in spheres other than the military, an increase in the international financial resources available to meet balance of payments and debt rescheduling problems is a prime area of opportunity.

In the same context, early and serious attention should also be given to achieving a new general agreement among the OECD nations to increase substantially the replenishments of the World Bank's soft loan IDA window. As a corollary, it is in the long-term interests of the United States to encourage IDA to give greater emphasis to long-term infrastructure projects, especially in the transport sector in sub-Saharan Africa. Like higher IMF quotas, such a program would encounter stiff political opposition in some of the donor countries, notably the United States. But this could be overcome by demonstrating the long-term U.S. self-interest involved in "investing" in the future.

The Private Sector Role

The emphasis given in the previous section to international institutions as instruments through which the United States can address the mutual long-term interests it shares with Africa is not intended to minimize the significant role that banks and corporations should be encouraged to play. Indeed, as noted earlier, one of the stronger arguments for enhancing IMF capabilities is that it would encourage U.S. banks and corporations to remain involved in Africa.

An assessment of *United States Participation in the Multilateral Development Banks in the 1980s* issued by the Department of the Treasury in February 1982 argues that the multilateral development banks (MDBs) must be approached as institutions that encourage the participation of developing countries in the Western economic system on a permanent and self-sustaining basis. Accordingly, the document concludes, future U.S. support for the MDBs should be "designed to encourage" the following:

— *Adherence to free and open markets,* on the grounds that this maximizes economic efficiency and encourages self-sustaining development. . . .
— *Emphasis on the private sector as a vehicle for growth* through innovation, risk-taking, adaptation of technology, and efficiency in resource use, in order to improve the economic prospects of developing countries.
— *Minimal government involvement,* to permit concentration of limited administrative capacity of LDC governments on functions that are essential, such as provision of "public goods"; distributing the benefits of, and imposing the costs of, external economies and diseconomies, respectively; and correcting identifiable market imperfections.
— *Assistance to the needy who are willing to help themselves,* in keeping with our historical tradition and

willingness to aid those less fortunate than ourselves.

This philosophical orientation requires that U.S. policy seek greater emphasis upon the MDB financial role as catalysts for private flows (the "banking" function) and their advisory role as sponsors of appropriate policies—as distinct from their significance as sources of official capital transfers. We should also emphasize the broader development role of these institutions, which lies primarily in the area of encouraging the most effective economic policies, including greater LDC reliance on market forces. Among the MDBs, *those to be most favored are those which are most effective at promoting economic growth and development.*[32]

The emphasis given in the Treasury document to encouraging a tilt by African borrowers toward Western economic (and implicitly political) models is not entirely consonant with the operating principles of U.S. corporations and banks active in Africa. The U.S. corporate presence can be found where there is business to be done—and that includes such avowedly "Marxist" states as Angola and the People's Republic of the Congo. Indeed, the *Wall Street Journal* in July 1980 featured a major article correcting misconceptions of Zaire, a "purportedly free capitalist country ... which is in fact a totalitarian state that seeks to control all economic activity above the subsistence level," while giving near-rave notices to "the purportedly communist country of Congo, which in fact has discovered the benefits of the free market [and appears to be] largely free of the corruption and routine restriction that plague Zaire."[33]

Equally instructive, for those who have a stereotyped view of U.S. corporations, is the February 1981 declaration of the U.S. Chamber of Commerce on Zimbabwe-U.S. trade and investment development. It urges action along the following lines:

1. American policy toward Zimbabwe should follow concrete national interests rather than ideological labels. While Zimbabwe's leaders espouse certain Marxist ideas, they have pursued policies of friendship with the U.S., peace with all their national neighbors, reconciliation among their own tribes and races, support for their own private sector, and openness to economic intercourse with the West. Their domestic income redistribution programs have been sound moderate efforts which, if successful, will eventually benefit all groups.

2. The new Zimbabwe regime represents the greatest defeat for the Soviet Union in Africa since Egypt's banishment of Soviet troops. The conditions established for the recent opening of a Soviet embassy in Salisbury underlined this fact. Britain trains Zimbabwe's army. The West enjoys most of Zimbabwe's trade. . . . On a continent where the U.S. often feels embattled, the U.S. should strongly support such a friendly, independent, potentially successful regime.

3. Zimbabwe possesses enormous economic potential. Its diversified minerals, agriculture, manufacturing and tourist industries combine with black Africa's finest administration and infrastructure to create the possibility of an economic takeoff comparable to those which have brought strength and stability to key American friends elsewhere.

4. The success of Zimbabwe's pragmatism would greatly influence Zimbabwe's neighbors. Already Zimbabwe's pragmatic economic policies are influencing Mozambique and Zambia, to the benefit of both those countries and the West. In the future, Zimbabwe's progress toward racial harmony could become a model for South Africa and Namibia.

5. Because of its economic potential, strategic position, and critically important minerals, Zimbabwe joins Nigeria as one of the two most important nations

in black Africa. America's policies and priorities should
focus on these two countries. . . .[34]

A more nuanced sense of the African political scene,
arising out of an increased experience on the continent over
the 20 years of decolonization, characterizes U.S. corporations and banks in the 1980s. Staffed by a new breed of political risk analyst (often drawn from the ranks of university-trained Africanists and former Foreign Service professionals),
the private sector institutions are beginning to provide a
continuity to U.S. relationships with African states and regions that will compensate in part for the quadrennial rediscoveries of the dark continent cited earlier as a problem
in government-to-government relations. Although no segment of American society is more intrigued than the corporate world with "the magic of the marketplace" that President Reagan emphasized in his September 29, 1981 address
to the Board of Governors of the World Bank and IMF, there
is also a recognition that some areas of acute African need
are ones into which multinational corporations are neither
equipped nor inclined to enter. Development of the rural agricultural sector and of intrastate and interstate transport
networks—both of priority importance to Africa's future
political and social stability—are cases in point.

Two other considerations that should temper the inclination of U.S. policymakers to condition assistance to African governments on a reduction of the public sector are the
prevalence of poverty in Africa and the long exposure of Africans to the public sector models of France and other Western European countries. In these circumstances, the United
States may conclude that it can best foster an environment
favorable to the nascent private sector by helping to make
the public sector operate more efficiently and cost-effectively—for example, by providing financial and technical advice
and managerial training suitable for state-owned industries.

Populist Time Bombs

Not only in "oil syndrome" countries but in others with *papier-mâché* state structures, economic resources are often used in ways that do not take the national economy forward and thus widen the gap between "haves" and "have-nots." In these circumstances, coups by individuals or groups espousing populist, puritanical anticorruption goals (such as Liberia's Master Sergeant Samuel K. Doe in 1980, Ghana's Flight Lieutenant J.J. Rawlings in 1979 and again in 1981, and the abortive Kenyan air force uprising in 1982) will continue to spark intense emotional support among the disadvantaged, at least in the early stages.

In countries with Muslim majorities, the restlessness of the have-nots may be channeled into some version of the Islamic fundamentalism that has become a major political factor in the Middle East. As recent developments in Iran and Egypt have demonstrated, the armed forces and educated technocrats are not immune from the frustrations and yearnings that propel Muslims into fundamentalist movements that would replace politicians or governments perceived as corrupt and elitist by a vaguely egalitarian (some would say anarchic) polity based on the teachings of the Koran. These movements inevitably have an anti-Western component, to the extent that corruption is identified with Western tendencies toward materialism and secularism.

As the 1980s get under way, African leaders are far more aware of and concerned about the existence of these populist time bombs than they were a decade ago, but the will to find ways of defusing them in nonrepressive ways is as yet spotty at best. Coherent economic development addressed to the needs of the have-nots as well as the haves would help.

4

U.S. Security Interests Reconsidered

In the nearly four decades since World War II, there has been little basic change in the U.S. military's view of Africa as an appendage of U.S. security interests in Europe, the Middle East, and Asia. The interventions in the Congo in the early 1960s and in Angola in the mid-1970s, as well as the post-shah priority being given to cultivating "proven friends" along the continent's northern and eastern perimeters, fall into this contextual framework.

Military Bases?

As of late 1982, the United States had no military bases in Africa—unless one counts Diego Garcia, the Indian Ocean atoll that the British government made available to the United States for a period of 50 years under the terms of a 1966 agreement.[35] Even this outpost 2,400 miles east of the coast of Africa has become a regular OAU agenda item. Although they are separated by 1,200 miles, Diego Garcia is claimed by Mauritius on the grounds that the two islands were governed during most of the colonial period as part of a single jurisdiction.

Although there are no U.S. bases in Africa, "standby base access agreements" have been negotiated with three states whose location makes them important to evolving U.S. military strategy in Southwest Asia—Morocco, Somalia, and Kenya. The only formal defense agreement, of 1940s vintage, is with Liberia.[36]

Risks To Be Considered

By accepting the assumption that the most important U.S. strategic interest in Africa in the 1980s is the continent's potential utility as a way station for the evolving RDF, U.S. decision makers are also faced with determining whether the United States has an obligation to defend the governments supportive of this outreach from what the military terms hostile interdiction. In reaching the decision, they would have to define what hostile interdiction means. For example:

• If the uprising of elements of Kenya's U.S. and Israeli-trained air force in August 1982 had succeeded or had seemed likely to succeed in overthrowing the elected government of President Daniel arap Moi, would this have been hostile interdiction requiring U.S. intervention?
• If Somalia's President Mohamed Siad Barre's government were to be unseated by a rival military-led group that was not overtly anti-Western but favored rapprochement with Soviet-supported Ethiopia, would this be hostile interdiction?
• Is the U.S. link with Morocco so tied to the institution of the monarchy that the United States would be obligated to preserve that institution at all costs?
• How far should the United States be prepared to go to

sustain President Jafar al-Numeri in Sudan, where some 2,500 U.S. troops with support aircraft were allowed to hold major military exercises in December 1982? An advance announcement of the exercises, which involved Oman and Somalia as well as Sudan, said that they were designed "to underline the U.S. ability to make good its pledge to support Middle East friends if they face an external threat." What is the line between an obvious external threat and an internal challenge that is believed to have, or may in fact have, some active outside support? And under what circumstances do we determine that a country located on the African continent is "Middle Eastern" and thus falls under a different set of guidelines than if it is perceived as African?

These questions need to be considered in all their dimensions by military planners and by diplomatic and area intelligence professionals to define in advance the choices with which national decision makers could suddenly be confronted—particularly in countries with a significant U.S. military presence and to whose leadership the United States may be perceived to be committed by those seeking to change the status quo. A related question is how much redundancy has been written into RDF logistical requirements.

South Africa

An argument of earlier times—that South Africa is the only African country capable during wartime of supplying its allies in the western Indian Ocean region with sophisticated industrial infrastructure support (factories, supply depots, repair facilities, dry docks)—remains factually correct. But few defense planners in the 1980s any longer push what used to be called—with reference to its important naval repair and supply facilities—"the Simonstown option."

The lower priority accorded southern Africa by today's

military strategists might seem anomalous in view of the domination of the world's strategic minerals market by South Africa and the Soviet Union and the presidential-level attention given by successive U.S. administrations to the significant Cuban and Soviet military presence in the southern third of the continent.

The evolution in the defense planners' thinking about South Africa's relevance to U.S. global planning has involved strategic, tactical, and empirical considerations, of which the following are illustrative:

• Changes in the global strategic and political environment since World War II have caused military strategists to reexamine some of the assumptions underlying the high priority that South Africa would have us attach to "the Cape Route." The case for the Cape route begins with the fact that more than half of Western European and a fifth of U.S. oil supplies pass around the Cape of Good Hope; a prolonged cutoff of these supplies by hostile forces operating in the area could have a severe impact on Western economies and Western security. A related assumption is that major political changes in South Africa placing in power a government friendly to the Soviet Union could lead to actual Soviet use of South African ports and airfields to interdict Western shipping around the Cape. The operational mandate arising from these assumptions is that the United States should support the present anti-Communist white government in Pretoria rather than engage in destabilizing pressures for change.

• An implicit assumption in the Cape route thesis is that a Soviet move to interdict the oil flow would lead to a conventional war of attrition on the World War II model. The growing strategic and tactical nuclear arsenals of East and West, as well as the developing rapid deployment capabilities on both sides, suggest a different scenario.

• Although the USSR has developed increased air and sea-lift capacity to project its own force or that of its allies into Africa, the prospect that the Soviets would employ this capability in southern Africa even at a time of extreme East-West tension to blockade Western oil supplies is discounted by many of today's military strategists on the grounds that any such Soviet move would be likely to initiate World War III.

• Recent studies by the U.S. Navy indicate that the Cape segment of Europe's oil lifeline is no more important or vulnerable than a number of other zones along the route, including the coast of West Africa, Madagascar, and the Mozambique Channel. The real choke points for Western oil supplies are at their source and destination—the Strait of Hormuz and the approaches to European ports. Focusing on the shipping lanes around the Cape would involve patrolling thousands of miles of often stormy seas in the South Atlantic.

• The Cape route thesis is also based, as Robert S. Jaster has observed in a recent study, on "woolly political thinking."[37] No African country except Somalia has yet granted formal base rights to the Soviet Union, and the agreement with Somalia became defunct when the USSR and the United States changed partners on the Horn in the late 1970s. The West African nation of Guinea has withdrawn the right it granted the Soviet Union in the mid-1970s to fly TU-95 military reconnaissance flights from its airfields. The Soviets have access to Angolan and Mozambican ports and airfields, but there are no permanent basing agreements with either of these states. Libya does not allow the Soviet Mediterranean fleet either port or refueling rights.

• The specter of a resource war involving blockage of the movement of southern Africa's strategic minerals to the West is based on some of the same assumptions about African behavior and Soviet behavior in Africa that provide the underpinning for the Cape route thesis. In fact, nowhere has a close relationship with Moscow resulted in Soviet pressure for a cutoff of economic relations with the West. In Angola, the most striking example of the avowedly socialist states' "open door" to Western economic investment and trade, the list of U.S. corporations and banks that continue to thrive include Gulf, Texaco, Mobil, Chase Manhattan, Citibank, First Boston, Bankers Trust, Boeing, Lockheed, and General Electric.[38]

• Military strategists and political analysts along a wide ideological spectrum in and out of South Africa and in and out of the U.S. government also have come to believe that South Africa is not on the verge of full-scale revolution. As William J. Foltz observed in November 1982:

> The government's repressive apparatus is too effective; the military has too much sway over neighboring states; the divisions within the white population do not yet seriously undermine the consensus on the necessity for white political domination; and above all the black population lacks access to the resources that might permit effective leadership to arise. Black grievances are such that the country may be in a "pre-revolutionary" situation, but it has been there for a long while.[39]

Change in South Africa seems most likely to follow a process that former U.S. Ambassador to South Africa William Edmondson has aptly called "violent evolution," with the most important sources of change ones that are internal to South Africa.

"In the absence of dramatic regional events," Foltz concludes, "the United States and the other Western nations will continue to deal with South Africa at arm's length, but deal with it nonetheless . . . [while the] Soviet Union's principal role for the moment seems to be that of useful support for [Pretoria's] 'total onslaught' ideology." Meanwhile,

South Africa's domestic and regional policies will continue to provide "helpful support for [the Soviet Union's] policy in the rest of Africa."

The bottom line appears to be that neither Soviet strategic planners nor U.S. strategic planners anticipate that South Africa's transformation is necessarily going to be apocalyptic or that the white monopoly of power is going to be significantly diminished soon.

More than five years ago, political-military affairs analyst William H. Lewis summed up the overriding military consideration in dealing cautiously with South Africa: "Quite aside from the political and moral issues involved, the prudent planner would not choose to have the United States locked into a dependency relationship with the South African military establishment if—or when—the Republic becomes a garrison state."[40] As Lewis notes, it is precisely for the same reasons in reverse that South Africa continues to take imaginative initiatives to woo Western nations into such a relationship.

Why Mozambique Matters

U.S. and Soviet strategic planners are probably correct in their assessment that apocalyptic change is not a near-term prospect within South Africa, but there is a regional phenomenon taking shape in southern Africa that could confront both Moscow and Washington with far-reaching decisions at any time.

Although there is by no means unanimity of opinion in South African power circles about regional strategy, developments in 1981 and 1982 indicate that the rationale of the "hawks" for a South African policy of regional destabilization is, for the present at least, operative *de facto*. Peter Vale, director of research at the South African Institute of International Affairs, provided a succinct summary of the hawks' position in a major Johannesburg newspaper in September 1982: "The rationale for a fairly ambitious policy of regional destabilization has a seductive logic. . . . Given that the Republic's neighbors are both military and economic dwarfs, the goal is to keep them that way and, in so doing, to ensure that Pretoria's hand is not removed from the tiller controlling regional events."[41] Without such a policy, the argument goes, the states around South Africa could achieve a degree of economic independence, perhaps through the nascent Southern African Development Coordination Conference (SADCC) launched in 1979, that would allow them to feel less constrained about permitting the African National Congress (ANC) to use their territories as springboards for cross-border guerrilla actions into the Republic. In the hawks' view, Pretoria's security interests are, as Dr. Vale phrases it, "best served by keeping these states cowed," and this end is served by "persistent involvement in their domestic affairs."

Consistent with this analysis of the regional situation confronting the Republic, the South African government defends its extensive military operations into Angola since the late 1970s as a legitimate carrying of the Namibian war to the bases from which the South West Africa People's Organization (SWAPO) guerrillas operate. South Africa's escalating covert support of the MNR in Mozambique is one of the world's least-kept secrets.[42] In other neighboring states the "cowing" takes other forms. The December 1982 raid into Lesotho's capital was justified as an act of self-defense against ANC "terrorists" alleged to be planning operations over Christmas in the Republic.

African governments tend to believe that the United States could, if it possessed the will, prevent South Africa from acting to destabilize its neighbors. Thus, the overthrow of the government of President Samora Machel by the South African-backed forces of the MNR could, as Professor Michael Clough of the Naval Postgraduate School postulates in a recent study, lead regional leaders to one of two conclusions:

> On the one hand, they might decide that U.S. leverage over South Africa is indeed limited, in which case the perceived advantages of cooperating with the United States, as African leaders have done in the Rhodesian and Namibian negotiations, would be greatly diminished. This would in turn significantly reduce the ability of American policymakers to play a constructive role in the region. On the other hand, African leaders might conclude that the United States in fact supported South Africa's activities. This would serve to confirm the contention that in the final analysis American governments will always side with the white regime in Pretoria and that therefore the struggle against apartheid will inevitably involve conflict with the United States.[43]

Either line of logic, both of which place the United States in a no-win position, could have a profound effect on South Africa's own black nationalists, and gravely hamper prospects for reformist change within the Republic.

The Soviet Union, whatever its priorities and preferences in Africa in the near term, might find it difficult not to respond to a request for assistance from a beleaguered Machel, because a failure to protect an endangered ally could seriously damage Soviet credibility throughout the continent and elsewhere in the Third World. If the Soviet Union or Cuba, or both, were to intervene at Machel's request to save his government from replacement by a regime beholden to South Africa, as Clough points out, they "would doubtless receive the blessing of the majority of African nations," as they did in 1975 when they came to the aid of the MPLA against South African military intervention in the triangular power struggle that marked Angola's independence and, again in 1978, when they supported Ethiopia against Somali irredentism. It has not escaped Soviet notice that two subjects on which all member states of the OAU can find common ground are opposition to South Africa and to efforts by fellow members to change African borders.

However ironical it may seem to argue that U.S. interests in Africa will suffer if Mozambique's Marxist government is overthrown, the reality is that viewing South Africa's destabilization of Mozambique in East-West terms could be as costly as the no-win situation in which the United States found itself when it viewed Angola through those lenses in the mid-1970s. Clough urges that the United States act on three fronts to keep the Mozambique situation from reaching a point where the Soviet Union might have no option but to intervene directly or with surrogates: Washington should "move quickly and decisively" to send the South African government "unambiguously worded public communications of American opposition to support for the MNR" and "give serious thought to discovering ways of increasing the cost to South Africa of maintaining its current course of action in the region"; "encourage Portugal and other West European nations to provide military assistance to Mozambique," in view of the fact that U.S. domestic realities "preclude any direct American military activity in this area"; and undertake a major commitment to the Southern African Development Coordination Conference (SADCC) plan to rebuild the region's transportation network to "provide indisputable evidence of U.S. willingness to support programs that enhance regional stability," even when those programs run counter to South African interests.[44] The question here is not one of supporting a "socialist regime" as such, but rather of finding ways of alleviating the insecurity of the leaders of all states of southern Africa and thus reducing the pressure on them to turn to the Soviet Union as the "natural ally" against South African hegemony.

Clough's implicit assumption is that the United States has the leverage, if it will but use it, to get P. W. Botha's government to see the ultimate self-destructiveness of the regional policy it is now following and to mend its ways. Given our track record with the far more dependent Israel of Menachem Begin—whose regional stance is the model for South Africa's hawks—it may take more than the United States alone can do to assure that Pretoria's "total onslaught" ideology does not indeed become fact.

Zaire

Since the U.S. intervention in the Congo (Zaire) civil war that followed the end of Belgian colonial rule in 1960, Washington has become increasingly ambivalent with regard to the country's "strategic" importance and the leader whom the United States helped to rise to power, President Mobutu Sese Seko.

This ambivalence was demonstrated most openly in Washington's responses to Shaba I and II—the invasions of Zaire's copper-rich Shaba (formerly Katanga) province by exiles resident in Angola in March 1977 and again in May 1978. As Professor Crawford Young, the dean of U.S. academic specialists on Zaire, recounts:

> At the time of the Shaba I incursion, Mobutu promptly accused not only Angola but also Cuba and the Soviet Union of instigating, arming, and equipping the invaders. The American response, officially described as "limited and measured," was a sharp disappointment to Mobutu, consisting mainly of accelerated supply of military equipment already in the pipeline. When it became clear that the FAZ [Forces Armées du Zaire] were incap-

able of coping with even this very small incursion, in mid-April Moroccan units with French logistical support intervened. The invading FLNC [Front de Libération Nationale du Congo] chose not to challenge the Moroccans, and melted back into Angola by late May.

Shaba II, in May 1978, had more extensive international repercussions, especially as the FLNC this time captured the copper-mining town of Kolwezi. Also, there had been important changes in the international context. Most importantly, the scale of the Soviet-Cuban intervention in Ethiopia shocked the West. In the United States, that portion of the policy community which viewed events through the prism of global strategies argued that Shaba II bore the hallmark of Soviet machinations, and required direct confrontation. . . .

Shaba I had established certain parameters affecting the decisions of external actors. . . . This time, the Western reaction was swifter, though divided. The most unequivocal support came from France, which quickly decided to dispatch the Foreign Legion, en route with American air transport by May 18. Belgian paratroopers were also involved, though with a more ambivalent definition of policy aims, centered upon rescue of the expatriate population. . . . And this time, in contrast to Shaba I, President Carter publicly echoed Mobutu's allegations of Soviet and Cuban complicity in the invasion, only to retreat from them in late June when it became evident that the CIA was unable to document them. However, there were much more widespread expressions of active support for Mobutu against the invaders. . . . An "African" force was quickly stitched together, to replace the French and Belgian troops; the main component was again Moroccan, but it also included token Senegalese, Togolese, Ivoirian, and Gabonese elements. . . .

The perception that the Mobutu regime is "propped up" by the West, and especially the United States, is well-nigh universal in Zaire (and for that matter throughout Africa). This perception became reinforced with the advent of the Reagan administration, which had pledged more active support to pro-Western regimes in Africa both during the campaign and in its early months in office. In fact, the actual change is probably less than the perception, though there has been an increase in military aid.[45]

Young shares the view of many Washington analysts that there is no very appealing policy alternative available. The efforts during the Carter administration years to demonstrate some distance while at the same time promoting political and economic reforms did not enjoy outstanding success. President Mobutu has thus far managed—by astutely sustaining the "Mobutu or chaos" thesis, reinforced by an emphasis on the importance to Western economies of Zaire's cobalt and other resources—to transform the very weakness of Zaire into an asset for the survival of his regime.

The scenario that would be most pleasing to Zaire's patrons and creditors in the West would call for Mobutu to prepare the ground for new national leadership (that is, groom a technocrat successor) and relinquish power voluntarily in the way that Senegal's Léopold Senghor transferred the presidency to Prime Minister Abdou Diouf in 1980 and Cameroon's Ahmadou Ahidjo stepped down in favor of Prime Minister Paul Biya in November 1982. Present evidence does not suggest, however, that Mobutu is thinking along these lines. From Washington's standpoint, the next best case transition might be a less bloody version of Master Sergeant Doe's takeover in Liberia in 1980—an elitist-to-populist shift involving no diminution and perhaps a strengthening of the U.S. role as patron. A worst case scenario, one following an Ethiopian or Iranian model, would result in a major reduction of Western influence, or even the expulsion of the U.S. presence.

Although France, Belgium, and the United States would exert a maximum effort to align themselves with whatever individual or group takes power after Mobutu, it is not at all certain that any alternative exists that can hold the country's disparate parts together for a reasonable testing period. Although Mobutu's route to prominence was through the Belgian-led *Force Publique*, it is doubtful whether the officer corps of today's FAZ would respond to Mobutu's demise with the coherence and sense of national purpose displayed by their Egyptian counterparts following President Anwar al-Sadat's death. A new factor with unpredictable ramifications is the escalating Israeli role in the training and equipping of Zaire's military since diplomatic ties between the two nations, severed by Mobutu in 1973, were renewed in May 1982. Unless there are major changes, however, it is not unlikely that Zaire, like nearby Chad, would splinter into several regionally based warring factions. The size of the country, which is comparable to the United States east of the Mississippi, and the deterioration of the rudimentary but effective transport network that linked key regions together during the colonial era add substance to this scenario.

If post-Mobutu Zaire comes to resemble the Zaire of the early 1960s, the introduction of a UN or other international peacekeeping force may once again be seen as the only means of preventing the Soviet Union and its surrogates from taking part in what could be a prolonged power struggle. The role of neighboring Angola would be critical at various junctures—which is another reason why settlement of the Namibian dispute and the related reduction or elimination of the Cuban presence in Angola is a priority U.S. interest. Zaire can no longer be perceived as an entity unto itself; by virtue of its proximity to Angola and Mobutu's pending bid for membership in SADCC, it should henceforth be viewed as part of the unfolding drama of southern Africa.

Why the OAU Matters

Although some disputes in Africa that are basically unfinished business from the colonial era cannot be resolved without the help of outside negotiators—Rhodesia/Zimbabwe in the 1970s and South West Africa/Namibia continuing into the 1980s—there are many interstate African issues that are in the U.S. (indeed, in everybody's) interest to keep in African channels. This warrants underscoring because of the inclination of U.S. policymakers to look for the East-West dimension of any ambiguous development on the continent. It is in this context that the role of the OAU warrants a more careful evaluation than it usually receives in U.S. policymaking circles.

For those of us who witnessed the contentious preliminaries to the OAU's founding in 1963, the fact that the organization has survived intact for 19 years is a remarkable achievement that few were prepared to predict at the outset or in some of the stormier years since. Volumes could be written (in fact, have been written) on the structural and functional weaknesses of the OAU, but both of these weaknesses were inherent in the compromises that had to be made at the founding conference in Addis Ababa between the differing conceptions of "unity" held at that time by the so-called Brazzaville-Monrovia and Casablanca groups. Given what the OAU is—an association with very limited power but possessing the collective moral clout to render certain specified kinds of conflict unacceptable—the organization's role is relevant to U.S. security interests on the continent.

When the boundaries of Africa's more than 50 political entities were devised at European bargaining tables in the nineteenth century, the shapes, sizes, and arrangements of the various colonial territories were not determined by geographic, ethnic, linguistic, or economic considerations related to any notion of their ever becoming self-governing states. Nevertheless, when decolonization of Africa began in the middle of the twentieth century, independent Africa's first generation of heads of state concluded that a Pandora's box would be opened up if any attempt were made to redraw the map inherited from the colonial era.

Thus, in Article III of the charter adopted at the founding conference and in various reaffirming actions taken since, the governments of independent Africa have maintained a high degree of consensus on two points: First, borders of member states at the time of independence remain inviolable in any OAU consideration of territorial disputes. Second, the OAU cannot condone any activities that are aimed at subverting governments of member states or any form of interference by one state in the internal affairs of another. Deviations from these two principles have been dealt with by the OAU, sometimes explicitly and sometimes by indirection, as breaches of the charter. (Several instances were Somalia's 1977–1978 military campaign to establish sovereignty over the Somali-inhabited Ethiopian province of Ogaden; the Eritrean, Biafran, Katangan, and southern Sudanese secessionist movements; Tanzania's 1979 military intervention in Uganda to assist in the overthrow of Idi Amin; and Israel's move into Egyptian territory.) The consistency of African consensus in this area, even in cases of misrule as flagrant as that of Uganda's Idi Amin, goes a long way toward explaining why no African state has lost territory to a neighbor's irredentism since 1963 and why no separatist movement has yet achieved its goal of establishing a new political entity. Moreover, no state—even one as shattered as Chad became in the course of its long civil war—has yet lost its "statehood" in the eyes of the OAU.

A clear differentiation must be made between the brake imposed by the OAU on irredentism and cross-border wars and the periodic flaring of disputes over borders imprecisely demarcated, especially when such border areas are found to contain potentially valuable minerals or oil. Also falling outside the OAU domain have been the responses by neighbors to requests from *recognized* governments for aid in quelling insurrections, such as Morocco to the aid of Zaire during Shaba I in 1977 and Shaba II in 1978, Senegal to Gambia in 1981, Guinea to Sierra Leone in 1971, or, by the OAU's implicit interpretation at its 1981 annual summit in Nairobi, Libya to Chad in 1980. Covert relationships between African governments and antigovernment forces in neighboring states inevitably remain another gray area.

An assessment of the role of the OAU should also note that the annual gathering of the continent's presidents, prime ministers, and foreign ministers has been more than ritualistic. Decisions have sometimes been fuzzy, the rhetoric excessive, and the follow-through variable. But mountainous differences and misunderstandings have been worn down to molehill proportions, and African opinion on various issues has often been crystallized, in these marathon sensitivity sessions.

Libya's Qaddafi was engaging in rhetorical excess when he cited "systematic lobbying" and "bribes" by the United States as the reason for the lack of a quorum that forced postponement of the OAU's nineteenth annual Assembly of Heads of State, which he was scheduled to host in Tripoli in August 1982. Some states declined to come to Tripoli because of bilateral problems with Qaddafi. But the principal cause of the large-scale boycott was the questionable legality of Secretary General Edem Kodjo's February 1982 action admitting the self-declared Saharan Arab Democratic Republic of the disputed Western (formerly Spanish) Sahara to full membership and a seat at the 1982 summit.

Quite independently of Qaddafi's charges, however, there has been a developing groundswell of opinion, even among African moderates, that the laborious OAU efforts toward a negotiated settlement of the conflicting claims to the Western Sahara would not have gone off the track if the United States had not taken Morocco's side and implicitly recast the dispute in East-West rather than regional terms. There is lingering resentment, too, of the statement issued by the Department of State following the June 1981 eighteenth annual OAU summit in Nairobi reprimanding the African heads of state for their decision to reconfirm the previous designation of Libya's capital as the site for the 1982 summit—and thus the routine accession of the host country's head of state to the 1982–1983 chairmanship.

With the collapse of a second attempt to convene a quorum for the summit in the Libyan capital in November 1982, it will require a major feat of African shuttle diplomacy to get the organization back on track so that it can hold the planned celebration marking its twentieth anniversary in 1983. If the OAU manages to work its way out of its 1982 vicissitudes, the United States should henceforth shape its attitude and policies toward the organization in terms of a cup half full rather than half empty.

5

Is a Coherent Africa
Policy Possible?

A Nigerian novelist who recently returned to his home-
land after spending more than 20 years in the United States
has been sorting out his impressions of the American psyche.
Referring "mainly to American institutions" rather than to
Americans as individuals, T. Obinkaram Echewa writes:

> Americans apprehend rather than comprehend ideas.
> They do not have the discipline or the endurance to wrap
> their minds around a thought. Instead they prefer to
> grab, snatch or make a stab at it. Their mental energies
> are usually exerted as pulses rather than as continuous-
> ly flowing force. Americans tend to be direct and literal
> rather than allusive and figurative, stark rather than
> subtle. They are happier dealing with statistics than
> with nuances. . . .
>
> If you give an American child a package, he will
> quickly tear off the wrappings. If he finds a toy inside,
> he will start to play with it immediately. He will play
> feverishly for a while and then discard the toy out of
> boredom. Later, he might take it apart to see what makes
> it go. By contrast, a traditionally reared African child is

inclined to savor the mystery of what is inside the package for some while. When he eventually uncovers the toy, he will play with it only a little at a time, so as not to use it up.[46]

Mr. Echewa has struck close to home. The episodic pattern of U.S. policy toward Africa since World War II cannot be understood, much less corrected, unless it is viewed as part of a broader American inclination to approach problems in the foreign policy realm as elsewhere with a task force mentality. Thus, the major U.S. commitments of senior-level attention in Africa to date—to Zaire in the 1960s, to Angola and Rhodesia/Zimbabwe in the 1970s, to the current Namibia negotiations and the campaign against Libya's Mu'ammar al-Qaddafi in the 1980s—have all been approached as missions that were expected to have a definite beginning and end. One reason we have not yet developed a clear set of guidelines on U.S. interests and diplomatic objectives in Africa is that the U.S. government lacks either a policy planning or intelligence component focused on broad historical goals, realities, and options.

Intelligence Is Not a Dirty Word

For many Africanists in American universities and other nongovernmental institutions, intelligence is synonymous with "dirty tricks." The two most convincingly documented covert operations of the Central Intelligence Agency (CIA) reinforcing this stereotype with regard to Africa have been the anti-MPLA operation in Angola, halted by the Congress in January 1976, and the role played by the CIA in 1960–1961 in the coincidental rise to power in the recently decolonized Belgian Congo (Zaire) of a young colonel named Mobutu and the death, under mysterious circumstances, of the country's first prime minister, Patrice Lumumba.[47] But there is another facet of intelligence—research and analysis—that could be of pivotal importance in gradually developing a working consensus on U.S. interests in Africa.

In a political system such as ours, where changes in senior and even upper middle level policymaking positions are kaleidoscopic and, as noted earlier, the amount of substantive consultation that takes place with each new episode of musical chairs is often governed by such factors as personal style or partisan political considerations, the institutional memory of regional careerists is (or should be) a critical bridge.

As Sherman Kent, a Yale historian who played a major role in the Office of Strategic Services in World War II and subsequently returned to serve for 20 years as director of the CIA's Office of National Estimates, observed in a 1949 study of the relationship between strategic intelligence and U.S. foreign policy, the task of collecting and analyzing the many pieces of information that interact to define or affect U.S. interests throughout the world is "a specialty of the very highest order," quite different from line duty in either the diplomatic or military service. Intelligence, as defined by Kent, is "the kind of knowledge our state must possess regarding other states in order to assure itself that its cause will not suffer nor its undertakings fail because its statesmen and soldiers plan and act in ignorance." Although some of this knowledge may be acquired through clandestine means, "the bulk of it must be had through unromantic open-and-above-board observation and research."[48]

Ray S. Cline, former deputy director of CIA for intelligence, views Kent's book as a seminal work that "provided a generation of intelligence officers with a rational model for their profession of collecting and analyzing information," but cautions that some language suggesting that the author was describing an existing organization is misleading. What

Kent outlined was "an idealistic concept" that drew heavily on the role of the Research and Analysis (R&A) branch of the wartime OSS.[49]

To find a unit resembling Kent's "idealistic concept" in the postwar period, one must go back to the 1950s, when the R&A branch of the dismantled OSS had been spun off to the Department of State as a new Office of Intelligence Research (subsequently retitled the Bureau of Intelligence and Research—INR). The INR of that time left "current intelligence" and "morning briefings" to the operating bureaus and the executive secretariat. Its mandate, to which the unit's early leadership and staff of analysts clung with something approaching religiosity, was to lay out trends, to ascertain and describe basic forces and movements, and to define the possible long-term outcomes of alternative policy courses available to *all* those involved in a given situation. The INR of that era had (and wanted) no more than a token presence at the Secretary of State's morning staff meetings and considered it a major tactical victory when senior decision makers were occasionally shaken by career analysts' then-heretical counsel (such as, "Islam is not necessarily a barrier to communism," "neutralism is the wave of the future," "the French cannot win in Algeria," "the Baghdad pact is a loser," or "you may be able to put the shah back on the throne in Iran, but there will be another Mossadeq, or worse.")

The integrity of the contribution of such a service—wherever in the bureaucracy it is located—depends on a blend of respect for scholarship and nonpartisan Washington savvy in its leadership, relative isolation from the overheated atmosphere that surrounds the process of dealing with day-to-day policy questions, and staffing by men and women who expect to spend their lives, in or out of government, honing their understanding of a particular society or region. Although a good case can be made for the dangers of overidentification with one's area of responsibility in the implementation of policy, the policymaking process is well served by some kibitzers with long memories and a commitment to understanding rather than judging human behavior.[50]

An unsettling reminder of conclusions that can be reached concerning U.S. interests in Africa when contextual analysis is missing came across my desk recently in an unclassified African overview of Pentagon origin. "Morocco," the author stated flatly, "is our only friend in Northwest Africa." Aside from the matter of Tunisia, which, conceivably, was excluded as being in north-central rather than northwest Africa, where was the author of this declaration when Algeria's foreign minister played the key role in securing the release of the U.S. hostages held in Iran? And what do we do with the fact that the United States is Algeria's major trading partner, importing more of that nation's oil than any other customer?

As veteran analyst William H. Lewis reported in March 1982: "What dismayed Algerian policymakers [about U.S. policy toward their country during Secretary of State Alexander Haig's tenure] was the disregard for the intricacies and historic roots of North African political relationships and stresses, the rigidly East-West interpretation placed on the Saharan war, and the slighting of Algeria's posture and sensitivities demonstrated by the singlemindedness with which Washington has pressed for stepped-up military collaboration with Rabat."[51]

Any serious analysis of the complex of regional and superpower forces at play in northern Africa must reach the conclusion that the interests of the United States (and, coincidentally, the Soviet Union as well) are best served by a balance of power in the region—that is, a relationship among Morocco, Algeria, and Libya in which none of the three becomes predominant. If the U.S. military had to make a choice, wouldn't it accord greater importance to keeping the Medi-

terranean coastline free of Soviet bases than to the useful
but not absolutely critical logistical support for the nascent
RDF that Morocco's King Hassan II is providing in exchange for arms needed to continue military operations in
the Western Sahara?[52]
      To ask these questions is not to suggest that the United
States should downgrade its long-standing friendship with
Morocco; rather, it is to emphasize that U.S. interests in Africa are best served if the United States does not conclude
that friendship with Morocco precludes amicable economic
and political relations with its neighbors.

Policy Planning for Tomorrow as Well as Today

Although the Department of State's Policy Planning Staff
has brought some creative minds to the higher echelons of
government over the past 35 years and has added an important dimension to the policymaking process under some administrations, the co-option of this unit into day-to-day operations is the rule rather than the exception. We have to go
back to the early postwar years to find a time when a secretary of state (George C. Marshall) and his director of policy
planning (George Kennan) have been committed in both
word and deed to the principle that the policy planning role
should be future-oriented, nonoperational, and accorded
critical importance.
      Ideally, the director of policy planning should be a re-
spected and seasoned authority on international affairs
whose writings have been relatively nonpartisan (or at least
nonpolemical). This is no job, however, for an academician of
ivory tower bent. The effectiveness of the operation would
be heavily dependent on the administrative and networking
wizardry of both the director and his area officers in seeking

out and drawing on the lodes of expertise regarding various geographical and functional areas that are tucked away in corners of the government bureaucracy, in academic institutions here and abroad, in other governments, and among the political risk analysts of corporations.

Such a policy planning staff would be a major customer, of course, for the institutional memory bank discussed earlier as a crucial need in the intelligence community. Unlike the envisaged intelligence unit, however, the policy planning unit proposed here would have to be sensitive to the complex interplay of the legislative and executive branches of the government, various power centers within these branches, personalities, interest groups, and domestic political issues in shaping U.S. foreign policy in the short and long run on any given issue. It would also have to accept as a fact of life the educational function implicit in Dean Acheson's reflection that "it is our sad destiny to put people in the presidency with no experience in foreign affairs."

Ironically, Africa will only take on an identity of its own in the making of U.S. policy when or if an institutionalized advisory group comes into being that has as its sole mandate the determination of how or whether the jumble of perceived U.S. interests and priorities around the globe will fit together a decade or two decades hence. Without such a conceptual framework, Africa policymaking will remain, as it has since World War II, primarily an adjunct of U.S. security interests in Europe, the Middle East, and Asia.

Lessons from the Past

If the intelligence and policy planning capabilities envisaged here were in place, the predictable guidance for decision makers would be to avoid setting up rigid demarcations between "proven friends" and "anti-Western" non-friends. The problem with boxing and labeling African states as good guys and bad guys, as both the United States and the Soviet Union should have learned from their respective experiences in the relatively short time they have been involved in the political affairs of the continent, is that the kinds of boxes and labels devised in either Washington or Moscow tend to disintegrate in the African sun. The French and the British rarely make this mistake, which is a major reason why they so seldom find themselves out on a limb when a given African scene shifts suddenly.

Three perspectives on the risks run in stereotyping African leaders are instructive:

1. In 1969, a young army colonel named Jafar al-Numeri came to power by military coup in Sudan and formed a coalition government in close alliance with the Sudanese Communist Party. By 1970, the U.S. diplomatic presence had been reduced to an "interest section" level, and the educational system inherited from the British was being drastically restructured by ideologues of the Left. In 1971, the Communist component of the regime organized another coup aimed at displacing Numeri and transforming Sudan into a state organized along unambiguously Marxist lines. Although some 30 officers loyal to Numeri were liquidated, the takeover foundered. Much of the credit goes to Mu'ammar al-Qaddafi's Libya, which forced down the BOAC plane carrying the newly proclaimed head of state and his aide to Khartoum from London. Libyan authorities promptly handed the captives over to Numeri, who had in the meantime regained power as the result of a second uprising that brought the new Communist regime to an end three days after it had taken power. In 1982, for a complex of political and economic reasons that are essentially domestic, Numeri followed

the U.S. lead in denouncing Qaddafi as Sudan's major external enemy, and Sudan was second only to Egypt in the hierarchy of recipients of U.S. military and economic assistance in Africa.

The Moral: Just as it was premature to box and label Sudan as "lost to the West" in 1970, so we should be wary of making the assumption that the present close association with the United States is etched in stone. As Colin Legum, dean of Britain's Africanist journalists, has often said:

> Those who characterize African governments or movements as being pro-Western or pro-Soviet almost always do so out of a failure to understand why certain African leaders, governments, or movements find it useful to choose a particular foreign ally at a particular point in time. These relationships are largely transient, both because most African governments are short-lived and because the central thrust of continental politics (despite some aberrations) is still toward nonalignment. . . .[53]

2. In the case of President Anwar al-Sadat of Egypt, it is now argued that he focused so much of his attention on developing his image as a "proven friend" of the United States that he lost touch with his own people. Mohamed Heykal, the outspoken former editor of the Cairo daily *al-Ahram*, said in an interview with a U.S. correspondent in February 1982: "I don't mean to be rude, but you [Americans] killed him. . . . He was addressing himself to you, the Barbara Walters of this world, the Walter Cronkites of this world. . . . The friendship with the United States became a target in itself, not a means to achieve something."[54] The inclination "to count too heavily on an individual rather than on across-the-board relations with a nation's people" is viewed by Heykal as a "fatal flaw of American foreign policy."

3. Conversely, there is considerable evidence that the

pinpointing by the United States of its own special villains in the Third World may have just the opposite of the intended results. Tanzania's former Minister of Economic Affairs and Development Planning, A. M. Babu, addressed this phenomenon in a recent newspaper column:

> President Truman picked North Korea's Kim Il Sung as his arch-villain; . . . President Kennedy's nemesis was Fidel Castro; President Johnson's was Ho Chi Minh; President Nixon settled on Salvador Allende of Chile; and President Carter on Ayatollah Ruhollah Khomeini. Now President Reagan has his Qaddafi. All of these villains in one way or another challenged American policies in their regions, but none of them posed a serious security threat to the United States. Nevertheless, they have been presented consistently to the American public as if their power were deeply dangerous to U.S. survival and to world peace—and their removal essential for the good of humankind. . . .[55]

It is Babu's view that the publicity given to these individuals by U.S. presidents, and thus the world's media, was a significant factor in their becoming folk heroes throughout the Third World. In a similar vein, he notes the irony of the consequences of the 1956 effort led by "the Conservative Anthony Eden of England and Socialist Guy Mollet of France" to oust Egypt's Gamal Abd-al-Nasser over the Suez issue. Nasser emerged as the leading figure in the Middle East and Africa for more than a decade, Babu reminds us, while "both Mr. Eden and Mr. Mollet were thrown out of power in their own countries."

Nicholas O. Berry, writing in the *Christian Science Monitor*, explores at greater length some of the boomerang effects of the attention focused by the United States on Libya's Qaddafi:

By treating Libya and Qaddafi as international men-
aces, the United States reinforces Libyan bluster and
radicalism. The U.S. confirms that the mask is believed,
confirms that Libya is considered stronger than it really
is. . . .

[A]side from the intervention into Chad, which
risked little and served to enhance a radical image, Libyan foreign policy in practice consists largely of words,
tokens, asylum giving, monetary grants, guerrilla training, and foreign visits. It is a ceremonial, posturing, ideological, check-writing foreign policy. There is scant
physical commitment to reshape the region, much less
the world. Qaddafi truly believes in revolution, Arab
unity, and national liberation, but the extremes to which
he goes are pure theater. . . . The mask of strength had
to be created. For to transform a society is itself a weak-
ening process with its untried procedures, misallocated
resources, amateur managers, fragile communications,
and disgruntled traditionalists.

By threatening Libya with the Sixth Fleet, arms
to Egypt and Sudan, and callous musings on the elimination of Qaddafi, the U.S. dumps upon itself huge political and economic costs. . . . The entire Arab press, for
instance . . . condemned the U.S. role in the Gulf of Sid-
ra incident.[56]

How Much Diplomatic Manpower
Does Africa Warrant?

The demands put upon the U.S. diplomatic establishment
by the proliferation of African states in the 1960s prompted
Under Secretary of State George Ball to reply to an action
alert from Assistant Secretary for African Affairs G. Men-
nen Williams at the time of the 1964 Zanzibar coup with the
observation: "It is my impression that God watches every
sparrow that may fall; I do not see why we should compete

in that league.''[57] The implicit questions in the biblical para-
phrase are ones that still hang in the air in the higher reaches
of Washington officialdom: How much diplomatic man-
power does Africa warrant and aren't there some crises we
could leave to the former colonial powers to worry about?
The answer, as in the case of any question about Africa, is
complicated.

U.S. interests in Africa are indeed served by consultation on a regular basis with European allies whose roles on
the continent complement, long antedate, and are often
more important than our own. Although such consultation
is essential to any serious effort to evolve a more coherent
U.S. sense of purpose with regard to Africa, it is not a substi-
tute for direct, informed, and candid relationships with each
African state—regardless of size and ideological leanings.

When the United States deals with Africa, not as a superpower drawing the line against the Soviet Union, but
through on-the-ground envoys prepared by professional
commitment and experience to relate to host governments
on the basis of mutual respect and mutual interests, the basis is formed for a policy that can survive and adapt to whatever changes may lie ahead in any given country. The cost of
maintaining half a hundred diplomatic missions on the continent and surrounding islands is high (and is higher when
consulates are counted), but there are at least two practical
reasons for giving serious attention to the style and substance of each bilateral link in Africa.

The first is that Africa accounts for approximately one-
third of the total membership of the United Nations. One of
the characteristics of small governments is that they tend to
place great store in international organizations such as the
UN where, for example, a São Tomé or a Djibouti can, at least
in the General Assembly, have a vote equal to that of either
superpower. Even in the superpower-dominated Security
Council there is usually at least one African seat. For all its

imperfections, the UN remains a sounding board for the poor and the powerless—which, to a considerable degree, means Africa.

A second reason for maintaining a credible diplomatic presence in each African country is that, as the mini-war over the Falklands demonstrated in 1982, size and intrinsic importance do not necessarily determine where the spotlight will move in the restructured world of the late twentieth century. Nigeria is important to the United States by virtue of its size (an estimated one-third of the population of sub-Saharan Africa), its economic and political influence in the region and in the OAU, its position as the second largest source of U.S. oil imports, and the fact that it is making a second try at democratic civilian government under a constitution largely based on the U.S. model. For defense planners, geographical placement accords special importance to Somalia, Kenya, Morocco, and Sudan. From the point of view of those primarily concerned with the sophisticated and crucial communications facilities that had to be moved from Ethiopia when U.S. relations with that country foundered after the end of Emperor Haile Selassie's rule, the two most important countries in Africa today are Liberia and the tiny cluster of islands known collectively as the Republic of Cape Verde.

Whereas most African governmental changes evoke only yawns above the bureau level, occasionally the falling of a sparrow will send Washington into a state of acute agitation for reasons that border on the inexplicable to those unfamiliar with our folkways. For example, the two magic adjectives that generated an extraordinary mobilization of the U.S. military bureaucracy at the time of an abortive July 1981 coup attempt in the 4,361-square-mile West African republic of Gambia were "Marxist" and "Libyan-assisted." Kwesi Adu's commentary on Ghana radio, like most African analyses, dealt with the coup attempt as something less than a major East-West chessboard move:

One may not be far from right to say that the Gambia is the least likely place for an armed rebellion to take place. With a population of just over a half a million and almost surrounded by Senegal, it has until last week known political stability since independence in 1965. In fact, many refer to the Gambia as the Switzerland of Africa . . . a tiny population, virtually landlocked, and without a standing army. . . .

The Gambia, like most developing countries, has been facing very difficult economic problems. . . . Just as in 1979, agricultural production declined further and slumped to the lowest level in 30 years in the just-ended fiscal year. The severe decline in the country's main export crop, groundnuts, had an extremely adverse effect on the whole economy through a sharp decline in foreign exchange earnings. . . . Such a galaxy of economic problems, compounded by political issues, created a fertile ground for frustration and dissent to germinate.

One of such issues worth considering is the fact that Gambia, since 1965, has known no leader apart from [Alhaji Sir Dawda Kairaba Jawara]. . . . The very prospect of having a new face at Government House, coupled with new ideas . . . gave some sort of support for the rebels, at least at the initial stages of the uprising. This is a major lesson for many African leaders who think without them their countries cannot move. . . .

The least said about the role of Libya and other socialist regimes in the rebellion the better. Although the rebels were clearly of Marxist-Leninist orientation, there is no evidence that outside communists were involved. The earlier African leaders stop blaming every problem on outside interference and put their houses in order, the better. . . .[58]

Professionally staffed U.S. diplomatic missions in all African countries, in touch with all elements of society, are the best insurance available to us against misreading and overreacting to local crises and also against facing a crisis or opportunity with no cards to play.

Closing the Credibility Gap

One subject on which there is a broad consensus among Americans concerned with Africa is that the United States would not fare well in a poll taken to measure the credibility of the external powers playing a significant role in the affairs of the continent. The consensus breaks down, however, when credibility is defined.

Most recently during the Carter presidency (but also under President Kennedy in the early 1960s), the emphasis was on rhetoric and gestures calculated to convey a generalized sense of brotherhood and identification with African aspirations. Problems of credibility arose when rhetoric could not, owing to the complexities of the U.S. policymaking process, be backed up with explicitly or implicitly promised deeds.

For example, the idea of a mini-Marshall Plan for the Sahel that originated during a visit to West Africa by President Carter's mother had a brief lifespan, for the predictable reason that it had no chance of getting off the ground in a Washington where even routine foreign aid legislation moves through the Congress with increasing difficulty. Similarly, the one verifiable result of Vice President Walter Mondale's departure from his briefing book guidance following a meeting with South Africa's Prime Minister John Vorster in Vienna in 1977 (when Mondale replied to a reporter's question by agreeing that there was no real difference between the "full political participation" euphemism put forward in the talks and "one man/one vote") was that Mondale provided Vorster with a "duplicitous Americans" focus for the National Party's campaign in South Africa's November 1977 elections, enabling him to blur issues of genuine substance. Even many of the Americans and Africans who agreed fully with the Mondale statement were concerned that it could create unwarranted or at least premature expectations among South Africa's blacks that the United States would actively support revolution in that country. The analogous example of U.S. rhetoric vs. performance in the case of Hungary in 1956, along with the post-Vietnam syndrome still permeating the United States, were among the reasons for doubting that this was more than a tactical ploy undertaken in response to pressures of the moment.

Reagan administration spokesmen convey a different reading of the term credibility. Many months before he left academia to head the State Department's Africa Bureau in 1981, Dr. Crocker was making the case that "the current U.S. rhetoric aimed at assuring Africans whose side we are on is inappropriate and often counterproductive." Under guidelines of a policy option labeled "Concern for Credibility," he proposed in 1979 that the United States "approach Africa not as a suitor anxious to please, but on a less patronizing basis of shared mutual interest," a stance that would be "hinged openly and directly on a blend of U.S. global and regional interests."[59]

This posture also has its drawbacks, as Vice President George Bush learned in his November 1982 visit to seven African nations during which he sought to explain the logic of linkage between a Cuban departure from Angola and a Namibian settlement. Even President Daniel arap Moi of Kenya, categorized by the Reagan administration as a "proven friend" of the United States and thus the recipient of an increasing share of U.S. sub-Saharan aid, found it necessary for domestic credibility reasons to take strong public issue with the vice president on the grounds that making a Namibia settlement conditional on the Cuban troop issue served no

African interests except those of South Africa. U.S. credibility was also strained when the vice president, during his stopover in Zaire, pledged continued support of the "security and stability" of the country, and heaped what some would regard as excessive praise on President Mobutu for his personal courage, his sense of initiative in African affairs, and his resumption of diplomatic relations with Israel.

As noted in Chapter 4, the credibility of Washington's periodic affirmation of support for the "charter and foreign policy principles" of the OAU has been increasingly questioned in both Africa and Europe in the 1980s. Aside from the widely held view that U.S. statements and actions reinforcing Morocco's claim to the Western Sahara helped to scuttle a promising 1981 initiative for a negotiated resolution of the Saharan war, there are also second thoughts about the OAU peacekeeping force sent to Chad in late 1981 with substantial U.S. financial support. For example, A. M. Babu, writing in *Africa Now* of London in May 1982, assailed the United States and France for using "their diplomatic pressure and promises of financial aid to drag the OAU into taking a 'peacekeeping' responsibility which it had neither the means nor the experience to carry out efficiently and effectively [resulting in] a pathetic mess both within the organization and in Chad itself."

Washington provided Babu and like-minded Africans with more ammunition in an address by Assistant Secretary Crocker to the Baltimore Council on Foreign Relations in October 1982 that represented the OAU's Chad operation as a U.S. anti-Libyan success story:

> Our cooperative efforts with the OAU have paid off. For example, U.S. policy toward Chad, aimed at countering Libyan military adventurism, has yielded important dividends over the past 12 months. In 1980, 7,000

Libyan troops intervened in the Chadian civil war and quickly became a major source of regional instability, posing a direct threat along Sudan's border and creating great worry among the other states bordering Chad. Seriously concerned by the Libyan presence, we and others encouraged the Chadians to ask for Libya's withdrawal and to seek OAU help in solving internal problems. In late 1981, the then provisional Chadian government, headed by former President Goukouni, called upon Libya to remove its military force. We then worked closely with the OAU to prepare the way for an African peacekeeping force to maintain order in Chad once the Libyans left. . . .

For our part, the United States moved directly to facilitate and support this peacekeeping effort. We allocated $12 million to support the Nigerian and Zairian contingents with nonlethal equipment and to aid transport of supplies to Chad. We also supported OAU efforts to promote reconciliation among various Chadian factions. By June 1982, Goukouni, who refused reconciliation efforts proposed by the OAU, had been forced out of Chad and replaced by his principal rival, Hissene Habré. The OAU concluded that its troops could be withdrawn. For the past four months, Habré has consolidated his control over the entire country and actively pursued the goal of internal political reconciliation. . . . Chad's reconstruction and reconciliation must proceed apace if Libya is to be denied another opportunity for foreign meddling in a sensitive area. Recognizing this, the United States has just signed an agreement to provide $2.8 million in rehabilitation assistance over the coming year. . . .[60]

As the next month's developments revealed, the Chad crisis was not behind us. It was a split over seating of the Habré delegation that led to the aborting of the second effort to hold the OAU's nineteenth summit in November 1982.

Will the Real Voice of America Please Stand Up?

The image of U.S. values and interests projected to Africa is shaped not only by government-to-government policies and actions, but also by the content of Voice of America (VOA) broadcasts heard throughout the continent every day by those who own or have access to transistor radios. Controversy over the VOA's mission and content has persisted since its founding in the 1940s—a controversy that centers on whether the Voice should be viewed primarily as a pro-Western/anti-Communist propaganda vehicle, a journalistic venture following professional norms of unbiased world news and commentary, or a window on America, "warts and all."

In 1982, the VOA, which is part of the United States Information Agency (USIA), had a budget of $109 million, some 2,200 employees, and an estimated 104 million regular listeners worldwide for its 981 hours of broadcasts per week in 39 languages. Nobody jams the programs it beams to Africa, and a great many people listen, but extended empirical observation leads to the conclusion that the Voice makes certain flawed assumptions about the reasons Africans turn on their radios, what holds their attention, and what they believe of what they hear. Concerns about the relevance of the Voice fall mainly into three groupings:

• As a source of news and commentary, the Voice cannot compete with the British Broadcasting Corporation (BBC), which is an aspect of the British Empire on which millions of faithful listeners around the world hope the sun will never set. The BBC's reputation for reliability and integrity is so unique that African officials even in the socialist countries are likely to assume that visitors will want to join them in interrupting appointments when the BBC world news is due. The president of Djibouti assailed as "an ugly proposal and a bad governmental decision" a proposed cut-back in Somali-language broadcasts in 1981, and the *Washington Star* jumped headlong into the same "penny-wise, pound-foolish" parliamentary debate with an editorial noting that the BBC's external services "give a picture of the world that is universally recognized as about as close to objective truth as human reporting is likely to be."[61]

Although the BBC's external services are an important underpinning of British foreign policy and are nominally and budgetarily under the Foreign Office, the corporation has always looked upon these services "as the flagship of British culture and fairmindedness which produces incidental benefits for the nation."[62] The BBC's political editor, John Cole, notes that the overseas services "are jammed by totalitarian countries of right and left not because they tell lies, but because they tell the truth, and because they are believed."[63] This reputation has been built on a scrupulous dedication to independent and even-handed reporting, even when (as in the Falklands crisis of 1982) this has embarrassed British governments. In further contrast to the VOA, the BBC is wary of periodic efforts by the British government to strengthen transmission hardware when the moving spotlight of world attention shifts to new East-West hot spots (Afghanistan, Poland), on the grounds that any concentration of services on areas under Soviet pressure would provide support for the view that external services are part of a British propaganda machine.

• A significant portion of VOA's programming to Africa now consists of cultural and educational presentations. Books and other works on Africa are reviewed and excerpted at length, and much of the cultural content reflects a conscientious effort to appeal to specifically African or "ethnic" interests, and to educate. These programs are not without interest, but they are subject to credibility problems because they convey a much higher and broader interest level about Africa than in fact exists in the United States. And sufficient account is perhaps not taken of the fact that African radio listeners, like radio listeners in Tennessee or Oregon or New York, have a limited tolerance for uplifting educational fare.

• VOA's return, in the early 1980s, to what USIA Director Charles Wick describes as a more vigorous effort to counteract Soviet disinformation does not arouse the responses in Africa it may in some other parts of the world, because "the Communist menace" does not connect with African realities. It is easy for us to forget that Africans' experience with oppressive externally based masters has been entirely with West European colonial rule; to date, neither the Soviet Union nor Cuba has established a presence in an African country except by invitation and neither has yet declined to depart when asked to do so. In African eyes, moreover, the prospect of an overt or covert intervention by South Africa in an internal power struggle in an African state is perceived as a far greater long-term threat than assistance invited in by one side or the other from Moscow or Havana. South Africa's move into Angola in 1975 and Israel's taking of the Sinai in 1967 and its march to Beirut in 1982 are closer and more real than what has occurred in Poland or Afghanistan.

In a sense, the VOA is a microcosm of the unresolved ambiguities and discontinuities of the entire relationship between the United States and Africa. When Africans listen to BBC programs beamed to Africa, they know precisely what they are hearing—news and commentary calculated to be of interest not only to Africans but to everyone of whatever nationality or occupation who is living, visiting, or interested in Africa. They know that the BBC broadcasts in Britain itself, while the VOA is precluded by law from providing materials to U.S. radio networks and stations. When one turns to the BBC, there is a sense of listening in on the world that an African does not experience when he listens to VOA programs specifically crafted for African audiences. For these reasons, and because the "propaganda" content of VOA varies from administration to administration, Africans have no clear sense of the extent to which the content of what they hear is the official word of the United States.

The answer is that sometimes it is and sometimes it isn't. But who is to figure out for sure unless a given presentation is a verbatim transcript of a presidential or other major policy address? Some long-time students of this problem have suggested that the ambiguity could be resolved if the VOA output were clearly divided into two segments—an official record, on the one hand, of U.S. executive and legislative branch statements, actions, and studies relevant to Africans and those concerned with Africa, and, on the other hand, features drawn exclusively from a noncommercial public broadcasting medium such as National Public Radio. Such a menu, carefully labeled as to official and unofficial components, might be one additional building block to add to those proposed in earlier pages that could, in combination, develop a less episodic U.S. policy toward Africa.

Some Minimal Guidelines

Most European, African, and American analysts take the view that U.S. credibility problems in Africa stem largely from the erratic image created by the tendency of both Democratic and Republican administrations to devise and invoke "principles" to justify ad hoc actions that are often reactive and often dictated or at least shaped by domestic political or anti-Soviet considerations. As the *Wall Street Journal* commented in a 1978 editorial,

[T]he United States has approached Africa in a state of confusion verging on schizophrenia. We waver, hopelessly torn between our legitimate cultural, strategic, and economic affinities and a desire for popularity and moral rectitude. . . . In the end, we achieve neither rectitude nor popularity, or self-interest.[64]

Granted that consensus is an elusive foreign policy goal for a nation that displays its pluralism as flagrantly as does the United States, our best hopes of bettering our credibility score and furthering U.S. long-term (as opposed to transitory and localized) interests in Africa lie

- in getting the facts straight;
- in developing an institutional mechanism for determining what developments and trends involve interests that are vital or even important to the United States over the longer run;
- in consistently supporting African efforts to prevent or resolve regional conflicts that could escalate into direct or surrogate conflicts between East and West;
- in seeking to maintain access to resources and trading partners and dialogue with African leaders, whatever the shifting ideological commitments of the governments involved;
- in furthering, by keeping open lines of communication and influence with all people by whom the future of South Africa will be shaped, nonapocalyptic change toward a just society in that country;
- in adhering, in such matters as IMF loans and other forms of conditional multilateral assistance where the U.S. vote carries potentially decisive weight, to a firm set of universally applicable behavioral principles;
- in encouraging, with both practical and moral support, the development of the regional economic building

blocks envisaged in the Lagos Plan of Action drawn up at the first OAU economic summit in 1980;

• in being wary of making rhetorical commitments or threats whose implementation neither U.S. public opinion nor the U.S. Congress can be counted on to support;

• in operating throughout Africa as a positive force confident of our own values and worth rather than reactively to a Soviet presence that is an inevitable phenomenon of the post-colonial era.

Notes

1. Helen Kitchen, "Eighteen African Guideposts," *Foreign Policy,* no. 37 (Winter 1979–1980):71.
2. For a day-by-day account of this period, see "Evolution of a Policy: A Chronicle of Developments in U.S. Relations With Africa: May 1–July 10, 1978," *African Index* (Washington, D.C.), vol. 1, no. 1 (July 15, 1978).
3. Kitchen, "Eighteen African Guideposts," p. 76.
4. John Hughes, *The New Face of Africa* (London: Longmans, Green & Company Press, 1961).
5. W. A. J. Payne (who now writes under the name William A. Jordan III), "Through a Glass Darkly: The Media and Africa," *Africa: From Mystery to Maze,* ed. Helen Kitchen, Critical Choices vol. 11 (Lexington, Mass.: Lexington Books, D. C. Heath and Co., 1976), p. 219.
6. Flora Lewis, "The Restless Spotlight," *New York Times,* October 22, 1982.
7. For a summary characterization of the Africa constituency and statements by some of its principal spokesmen, see "The 'Afro-Centric' Perspective" in "Options for U.S. Policy Toward Africa," ed. Helen Kitchen, *AEI Foreign Policy and Defense Review,* vol. 1, no. 1 (1979).

8. Francis A. Kornegay, Jr., *Washington and Africa: Reagan, Congress, and an African Affairs Constituency in Transition,* a Habari Special Report of the African Bibliographic Center (Washington, D.C., 1982), pp. 35–36.

9. Congressional Black Caucus, "Statement on United States Foreign Policy," March 1981.

10. *Washington Star,* June 10, 1981.

11. Seth Singleton, "The Natural Ally: Soviet Policy in Southern Africa," *Changing Realities in Southern Africa: Implications for American Policy,* ed. Michael Clough (Berkeley: Institute of International Studies, University of California, 1982), pp. 187–188, 192.

12. *Ibid.*

13. Robert Legvold, "The Soviet Union's Strategic Stake in Africa," *Africa and the United States: Vital Interests,* ed. Jennifer Seymour Whitaker (New York: New York University Press for the Council on Foreign Relations, 1978), p. 179.

14. Gerald A. Funk, "Some Observations on Strategic Realities and Ideological Red Herrings on the Horn of Africa," *CSIS Africa Notes,* no. 1, July 1, 1982. Based on Mr. Funk's presentation at a conference on "Africa: Continuity and Change in the 1980s" held in Monterey, California, on May 1–2, 1982 under the joint sponsorship of the African Studies Program of the Center for Strategic and International Studies (CSIS) and the U.S. Naval Postgraduate School.

15. John K. Cooley, *Libyan Sandstorm: The Complete Account of Qaddafi's Revolution* (New York: Holt, Rinehart & Winston, 1982), p. 287.

16. Lieutenant General Olusegun Obasanjo, "Who Will Determine Africa's Destiny?" in "Options for U.S. Policy," ed. Helen Kitchen, *AEI Foreign Policy and Defense Review,* 1, no. 1 (1979): 72.

17. Wayne S. Smith, "Dateline Havana: Myopic Diplomacy." Reprinted with permission from *Foreign Policy,* no. 48 (Fall 1982): 171–172. Copyright 1982 by the Carnegie Endowment for International Peace.

18. See, for example, *New York Times* editorial of September 7, 1979.

19. Peter Calvocoressi, "French Lessons in Africa," *Sunday Times* (London), October 10, 1982.

20. "The Empire Stays Put," *Economist* (London), July 10, 1982, p. 66.

21. Russell Warren Howe, "Leadership Role in Third World Seen As Peking's Road to Power," *Washington Times,* October 19, 1982. See also Hobart Rowen, "China Leads the Poor," *Washington Post,* May 20, 1982.

22. George T. Yu, "Sino-Soviet Rivalry in Africa," in *Communism in Africa,* ed. David E. Albright (Bloomington: Indiana University Press, 1980), pp. 168–188.

23. *Financial Times* (London), November 1, 1982.

24. U.S. Central Intelligence Agency, *Communist Aid Activities in Non-Communist Less-Developed Countries, 1979 and 1954–79,* ER-80-10318U (Washington, D.C., October 1980), p. 14.

25. "Ethiopia: The Incentive of Western Finance," *Africa Confidential* (London), vol. 23, no. 21 (October 6, 1982):8.

26. David E. Albright, "Sub-Saharan Africa and Soviet Foreign Policy in the 1980s," draft contribution to CSIS' Soviet Studies Project on "Factors Affecting Soviet Foreign Policy in the 1980s."

27. For a sampling of different points of view on U.S. strategic minerals vulnerability and related implications for U.S. policy toward various controversial governments in the southern portion of Africa, see Robert A. Kilmarx, *Toward a Coherent U.S. Policy on Strategic Minerals: A Guide to the Facts* (CSIS Significant Issues Series, vol IV, no. 3, 1982); Galen Spencer Hull, *Pawns on a Chessboard: The Resource War in Southern Africa* (Washington, D.C.: University Press of America, 1981); Michael Shafer, "Mineral Myths," *Foreign Policy,* no. 47 (Summer 1982); U.S. House of Representatives, Subcommittee on Mines and Mining of the Interior and Insular Affairs Committee, *Nonfuel Minerals Policy Review* Part III (September 18, 1980: Serial No. 96-9) and *Sub-Sahara Africa: Its Role in the Critical Mineral Needs of the Western World* (Committee Print No. 8, July 1980); Leonard L. Fischman, *World Mineral Trends and U.S. Supply Problems* (Washington, D.C.: Resources of the Future, 1981); U.S. Senate, Committee on Foreign

Relations, *U.S. Minerals Dependence on South Africa* (Washington, D.C.: Government Printing Office, 1982).

28. Andrew M. Kamarck, "The Resources of Tropical Africa." Reprinted by permission of *Daedalus,* Journal of the American Academy of Arts and Sciences, vol. 3, no. 2 (Spring 1982):149–163, Cambridge, Mass.

29. *Ibid.*

30. In developing the section on oil, I am especially indebted to Major David C. Underwood, USAF, for allowing me to draw on his thesis, "West African Oil: Will It Make A Difference?" prepared in partial fulfillment of the requirements for his degree of Master of Arts in National Security Affairs from the Naval Postgraduate School in Monterey, California (December 1982). Major Underwood's country-by-country study will be published in full under the aegis of the CSIS African Studies Program in 1983.

31. From Dr. Adedeji's remarks at a discussion on "Africa's Economic Prospects," hosted by the CSIS African Studies Program, October 27, 1982.

32. Department of the Treasury, *United States Participation in the Multilateral Development Banks in the 1980s* (Washington, D.C.: Government Printing Office, February 1982), pp. 77–78.

33. Jonathan Kwitny, "'Communist' Congo, 'Capitalist' Zaire," *Wall Street Journal,* July 2, 1980.

34. U.S. Chamber of Commerce, "Zimbabwe-U.S. Trade and Investment Development Declaration," February 1981.

35. For an account of the rationale and steps leading to the Diego Garcia agreement, see William H. Lewis, "How a Defense Planner Looks at Africa," in Kitchen, *Africa: From Mystery to Maze,* pp. 287–289, 305–309.

36. See *U.S. Treaties and Other International Agreements,* vol. 10, part 2:1598.

37. Robert S. Jaster, *Southern Africa in Conflict: Implications for U.S. Policies in the 1980s* (Washington, D.C.: American Enterprise Institute Special Analyses series, 1982), pp. 21–23.

38. See, for example, Gerald J. Bender, "Angola: Left, Right & Wrong," *Foreign Policy,* no. 43 (Summer 1981):66.

39. William J. Foltz, "South Africa: What Kind of Change?" in *CSIS Africa Notes*, no. 5, November 25, 1982.

40. Lewis, "How a Defense Planner Looks at Africa," p. 295.

41. Peter Vale, "Hawks, Doves and Regional Strategy," *Star* (Johannesburg), September 3, 1982.

42. See, for example, "Mozambique: Havoc in the Bush," *Africa Confidential* (London), vol. 23, no. 15, July 21, 1982.

43. Michael Clough, "Mozambique: American Policy Options," *Africa Report*, November–December 1982, pp. 14–15. Mr. Clough is the African area coordinator and adjunct professor of National Security Affairs at the Naval Postgraduate School in Monterey, California.

44. *Ibid.*

45. Excerpted from Dr. Crawford Young's presentation in a session on Zaire at the conference on "Africa: Continuity and Change in the 1980s" held in Monterey, California, on May 1–2, 1982 under the joint sponsorship of the CSIS African Studies Program and the U.S. Naval Postgraduate School.

46. T. Obinkaram Echewa, "A Nigerian Looks at America," *Newsweek*, July 5, 1982, p. 13.

47. On the role of the CIA in Angola in the 1970s, see John A. Marcum, *The Angolan Revolution*, vol. 2 (Cambridge: MIT Press, 1978), pp. 257, 271, 273, and John Stockwell, *In Search of Enemies: A CIA Story* (New York: W. W. Norton & Company, 1978). The latter book, written by a former CIA operative, also contains the author's account of the circumstances surrounding Lumumba's death (pp. 10, 105, 236–237).

48. Sherman Kent, *Strategic Intelligence For American World Policy* (Princeton: Princeton University Press, 1949).

49. Ray S. Cline, *The CIA Under Reagan, Bush & Casey* (Washington, D.C.: Acropolis Books, Ltd., 1981), pp. 100–101.

50. This discussion of the role of INR in the 1950s originated in an address by the author at a conference at the Naval Postgraduate School in Monterey, California, in 1979 and was subsequently developed into Guidepost 6 in "Eighteen African Guideposts."

51. William H. Lewis, "Why Algeria Matters," *African Index*, vol. 5, no. 2 (March 1, 1982):5.

52. For further discussion of these options, see I. William

Zartman's presentation on "Scenarios for Morocco" in the proceedings of the September 1982 CSIS conference on "Strategic Response to Conflict in the 1980s," to be published in 1983.

53. Colin Legum, "African Outlooks Toward the USSR," *Communism in Africa,* ed. David E. Albright (Bloomington: Indiana University Press, 1980), p. 15.

54. From an interview with David Ottaway published in The *Washington Post* on February 20, 1982.

55. Babu, who now teaches at Amherst College in the United States, made these observations in a contribution to the *Sun* (Baltimore, Maryland), January 10, 1982. His column appears regularly in *Africa Now* (London).

56. Nicholas O. Berry, "The High Cost of Threatening Qaddafi," *Christian Science Monitor,* September 30, 1981.

57. George W. Ball, *Diplomacy for a Crowded World: An American Foreign Policy* (Boston: Little, Brown and Company, 1976), p. 223.

58. Ghana radio, August 6, 1981.

59. See Option 5, "Concern for Credibility" in "Options for U.S. Policy Toward Africa," ed. Helen Kitchen, *AEI Foreign Policy and Defense Review,* vol. 1, no. 1 (1979):50.

60. Chester A. Crocker, "Challenge to Regional Security in Africa: The U.S. Response," an address to the Baltimore Council on Foreign Relations (Baltimore, Maryland), October 28, 1982.

61. "Pennies, Pounds and the BBC," *Washington Star,* July 23, 1981.

62. "BBC and the Foreign Office," editorial in the *Financial Times* (London), June 29, 1981.

63. John Cole, "The BBC's War Over Words," *Washington Post,* May 19, 1982.

64. From an editorial in the *Wall Street Journal,* August 23, 1978.

About the Author

Helen Kitchen is director of the African Studies Program at the Center for Strategic and International Studies, Georgetown University. She directed the Africa Area Study of the Rockefeller Commission on Critical Choices for Americans from 1974–1976, and was editor of Vol. XI in the Critical Choices series, *Africa: From Mystery to Maze* (Lexington Books, 1976). Her other books include *The Press in Africa* (1957), *The Educated African: A Country-by-Country Survey of Educational Development in Africa* (1962), *A Handbook of African Affairs* (1964), and *Footnotes to the Congo Story* (1967).

Trained as a journalist at the University of Oregon, she began her career on the editorial staff of the *Reader's Digest* in New York and subsequently entered into African studies while living in Egypt. She has been editor of *Africa Report* magazine (1960–1968) and *African Index* fortnightly (1978–1982) and has recently established a new periodical, *CSIS Africa Notes*. In 1979, she was guest editor of Vol. I, No. 1 of the *AEI Foreign Policy and Defense Review*, in which she explored and documented six "Options for U.S. Policy Toward Africa." Her articles on African affairs and the U.S. policymaking process have appeared in a range of journals and newspapers in the United States and abroad. "Eighteen African Guideposts," published in the Winter 1979–1980 issue of *Foreign Policy*, has been widely reprinted. "Six Misconceptions of Africa" appeared in the Autum 1982 issue of the *Washington Quarterly*.

"From the very beginning," Lewis Nkosi has written of her work in a review published in the *Journal of Modern African Studies* (London), "Mrs. Kitchen has obviously understood her task as being to make some way through the sea of red herrings on which popular journalism feeds, remaining deeply conscious always of the fact that in Africa there are no easy answers. . . . [Her] approach remains subtle, vigilant, informed . . . forever probing, examining, analyzing, without doing what comes easiest to many people, that is, passing judgement."